*"Tomorrow is school
and I'm sick to the heart
thinking about it."*

DOUGLAS & McINTYRE, Vancouver

"Tomorrow is school and I'm sick to the heart thinking about it."

DON SAWYER

Copyright © by Don Sawyer, 1979

All rights reserved. No part of this book may be reproduced or transmitted in any form by any means without permission in writing from the publisher, except by a reviewer, who may quote brief passages in a review.

Canadian Cataloguing in Publication Data

Sawyer, Don, 1947-
  Tomorrow is school and I'm sick
  to the heart thinking about it

  ISBN 088894-228-1

  1. Sawyer, Don, 1947-   2. Sawyer, Jan.
3. Education - Newfoundland. 4. Teachers -
Newfoundland - Biography. I. Title.
LA2325.S29A3   372.9'718   C79-091028-4

Douglas & McIntyre Limited
1875 Welch Street
North Vancouver
British Columbia

Photographs by George A. Carleton
Jacket design by Jim Rimmer
Typesetting by The Typeworks, Mayne Island
Printed and bound in Canada by The Hunter Rose Company

To my mother, and in memory of my father.

ACKNOWLEDGEMENTS

I would particularly like to acknowledge Tom Wayman's assistance; without his encouragement I would have never begun this book, and without his editorial advice and constant support I might not have completed it.

I would also like to thank Trevor Mouland, Myrtis Guy, Gerald Guy, David Hicks, Bramwell Butler and Perry Butt for their invaluable contributions.

CONTENTS

1

"Not like any place you've ever been"

"Why are they all staring at us?" Jan asked, glancing nervously at the people lining the narrow dirt lane that wound through Hoberly Cove.

"I don't know," I mumbled, meeting the unswerving eyes until they were lost in the thick dust. "I guess we do look a little out of place—two city people driving through a Newfoundland outport in a blue SAAB with B.C. plates."

Uneasily I saw that the road ended just ahead: we would have to turn and run through the gauntlet again. I wheeled the SAAB around and assumed as sunny a smile as I could manage.

This time the number of people seemed to have grown. Four generations stood, shoulder to shoulder, each fixing us with expressionless stares. To us recent fugitives from the mainland, this collective scrutiny was terrifying.

"My God," Jan muttered, "What are we doing here?"

The unlikely series of choices that had led us to the small fishing community of Hoberly Cove on the coast northeast of Gander had begun, in 1969, with our decision to emigrate to Canada. I had entered a program in modern Chinese Studies at the University of British Columbia. A few months of struggle with the Chinese language had then started me wondering if any Canadian employer could use a bright young married man with a degree in Communication Arts and considerable background in Chinese philosophy and political science. Dozens of job-seeking letters, all fruitless, brought me to a startling realization: nobody really cared about my success in undergraduate studies, my scholarship, or even my terrific references. My efforts became more frantic as my letters worked their way east. I finally sent off a barrage of resumés to school boards in Newfoundland, a place I could only foggily envision.

One day in late August I received a phone call at my parents' home in Birmingham, Michigan, from Mr. Russell Taylor, Superintendant of Schools for Terra Nova Integrated School Board in Gander, Newfoundland. Mr. Taylor was prepared to offer both me and my wife teaching positions in the schools of the small community of Hoberly Cove; I was offered a post in the village's high school and Jan one in the elementary school. I was astonished. Not only had I never taught, I had never even had a class in education. Furthermore, my wife had completed only three years of university, though they were in education, and where *was* Hoberly Cove, Newfoundland, anyway?

I collected myself well enough to persuade Mr. Taylor to give us twenty-four hours to decide. Jan and I looked at each other blankly. "Well," she finally commented, "I'll go if we can get a Newfoundland dog." Having grown up in the United States, we found that the name of a dog breed just about exhausted our knowledge of the island that was to be our home for two years.

We dashed to the Birmingham Public Library, a fairly good one designed to serve an American middle-class community of 35,000 people. We were able to find only one source of information beyond encyclopedias: a 1949 issue of *National Geographic* featuring a piece entitled "Canada's New Province." Among pictures of boys selling snared rabbits, the row houses of old St. John's, and gnarled fishermen looking steadfastly out to sea from open boats, were observations that presented Newfoundland as a society of human penguins, a place made up of isolated colonies perched on snow-packed rocks, its members continually darting into the icy sea to seize the few fish that enabled them to survive.

The image was so chilling that, even considering the intervening twenty years, we were not convinced that the place would be habitable by frail mainlanders like us. Still, our options had shrunk alarmingly. We could either brave the unknown of a land shrouded in perpetual fog and raked by constant Atlantic storms or spend the winter writing more letters of application from my parents' house in Michigan. Newfoundland won out by a considerable margin. The next day, Russell Taylor was pleased to learn that he had filled two more vacancies.

Now we began to worry. We were setting out on a fairly long journey to a sparsely populated area in a 1963 two-cycle SAAB. In 1970 there were no SAAB dealers in all of Canada, much less Newfoundland, and few service station attendants who had heard of a car that needed oil in its gas tank. Even a master mechanic, we feared, would cover his face in horror at the first peek under the hood. But the fact that our transportation was less than practical was the least of our concerns. In seven days we were expected to be competent teachers in classrooms in a corner of North America that our local library had hardly taken notice of. We loaded the SAAB to the windows with our luggage, and on Tuesday began the long journey east.

I had made reservations to cross on the ferry from North Sydney, Nova Scotia, to Port-aux-Basques, Newfoundland, for that Friday night, thus giving us four days to drive to Hoberly Cove and get settled before school was to start on Wednesday. But a struggling and missing SAAB wrecked our schedule and it was not until the Saturday that we were able to drive on to the ferry.

The trip stretched into a fourteen-hour purgatory as high winds and rough seas delayed docking at Port-aux-Basques. Except for the first hour, when we were still in the relative calm of the offshore waters, I was horribly ill the entire time. I lay in my narrow bunk in the ferry's churning bowels, my head lolling weakly from side to side with each roll of the vessel. Late in the evening I finally lapsed into a fitful sleep.

During the night the wind slackened and we were awakened by the sounds of docking and the crackling intercom. We hurried to our car and were the first off the ferry, landing in a soft rain on Newfoundland soil at 3:30 Sunday morning.

Anxious to be off, we sped northeast along the Trans-Canada highway. This is the route that did for Newfoundland what the CPR had done for Canada; the Trans-Canada Highway is not merely the main road across the island, it is the only road. Because we were travelling on such a major route, I didn't worry that my tank was only half full.

There were no gas stations along the way, at least no open ones. Signs promising service centres in twenty or thirty miles lied time after time: either they were not there at all or they were closed and cold. We pushed on through forests, over mountains, seeing only two cars on the entire lonely stretch of road. Finally, going up a mountain, I heard the ominous clacking of our fuel pump; we were running out of gas. I managed to nurse the car over the last crest and down the winding slope. We coasted, twisting for miles among the hills, then rounded a final curve at the very bottom of the mountain and glided slowly up to the pumps of an open Esso station. The attendant confirmed what we had already guessed—that this was the only open station between Port-aux-Basques and Corner Brook.

We continued east through the desolate stretches of bog land and scrub spruce that cover much of the interior of the island, and finally at 1:00 p.m. arrived at the Gander intersection. We followed the signs until shopping plazas appeared on either side of the road. Thinking that these were suburban malls, we drove farther, but found only blocks of military-looking subdivisions and barracks. This was Gander, the fourth largest city in the province, the site of an international airport, the hub of northeastern Newfoundland.

We phoned Russell Taylor, who suggested that we get a room for the night and come over to his house the next day. At the Albatross Motel Jan eagerly thumbed through the thin phone book that apparently contained every community on the island outside of the Avalon peninsula. Under "Hoberly Cove" there were about 150 names listed, and nearly half were Pritchett. Another quarter were Filliers and the remaining names were divided among three or four smaller clans. "Well, it won't be too hard to remember the kids' last names," Jan commented.

The next afternoon we visited our district superintendant and his family. Meeting Russell Taylor was reassuring. He was a tall, thin man, slightly balding, who radiated self-assurance and poise. He seemed efficient and somewhat aloof, yet also warm and sensitive. His tone in describing the situation in Hoberly Cove was guardedly pessimistic. "The place is ten years behind any other school in the district. I don't think you'll have much luck dragging it into the twentieth century. Still, there's a young American and his wife there who are trying some things, and a girl from Ottawa we've just hired. Maybe you can reinforce each other."

I asked him something that had been on my mind since we first received information on Newfoundland schools. "What exactly is an Integrated School Board? What or whom does it integrate?"

"That's rather involved," he began. "You see, until two years ago there were no public schools as such. All schools in the province were denominational, in that they were affiliated with different churches, received their funding through the denominational boards, and were subject to varying degrees of control by the churches. Students, then, were segregated by church affiliation. Hoberly Cove is staunchly Protestant, as is most of the northern coast. The south coast, of course, is mostly Irish Catholic. Anyway, the community is primarily Salvation Army."

I must have looked startled. "You mean the Salvation Army is the main church for the entire community? I thought they ran missions and secondhand stores."

"Not in Newfoundland," Russell said. "Here, the Army is one of the four largest denominations in the province. The high school and elementary school you'll be working in were originally Army schools. This was part of the problem. Many of the teachers in the schools were chosen because of their church affiliation rather than any particular talents as teachers.

"At any rate, two years ago several of the denominations hammered out an agreement which provided for the establishment of a non-denominational educational board that incorporated representatives from the different churches. This board, rather than the denominational boards, funnelled provincial funds to the various schools, allowing them to amalgamate and provide more extensive facilities and more efficient organization. You can appreciate the problems of a small town with three or four denominational elementary schools. Often none of them had enough students to support a full staff, so two or three teachers in each school would teach six, even eight grades.

"Anyway, an integrated board is one which is not controlled by a single denomination but incorporates most of the former Protestant boards. The denominations did maintain certain minimal jurisdiction over their former schools, however. In the Army's case, the most contentious issue has been its insistence on banning any dancing in the high school."

"That's incredible," I blurted. "I haven't heard of anything like that happening for twenty-five years."

Russell looked at me sharply. "Listen to me. The community you're going to is not like any other place you've ever been. There are good and bad things about it, but don't expect to evaluate it in terms of your past experience. Go in with the idea of its uniqueness and understand that the community as a whole, and particularly the schools, are caught in the middle of a sudden, difficult period of change. Do what you can, based on the situation as you find it.

"You know about the public exams, don't you?" Russell continued. Not sure of what aspect of these he was referring to, I had to shake my head.

"Well, until last year all students in grades nine, ten and eleven had to take standardized provincial exams to pass the grade."

Surprised, I could only ask about grade twelve.

"We don't have grade twelve here. Eleven is matriculation, a

6

carry-over from British junior and senior matriculation, most likely. Now only elevens must write public exams. The effects of withdrawing the exams have been traumatic for some teachers."

I was genuinely puzzled. "Why should that cause so much consternation? It seems to me that it would be a relief to be free of the exams."

"You have to realize," Russell said, "that for many teachers their entire training, experience and educational philosophy has centred around public exams. Everything—curriculum, tests, student and teacher roles, passing and failing, course offerings and so on—was a direct outgrowth of the public exam system. There was little opportunity for originality or imagination—it simply was not rewarded on the part of student or teacher. As you can imagine, the dropout rate, especially in the outports, was staggering. A fifty per cent failure rate in an outport school was not unusual."

"And this just changed last year?" Jan asked incredulously.

"That's right. Of course this won't affect you as much, but even in the elementary schools teachers argued that they had to begin to prepare students for the public exams. One result has been teachers who, often through no fault of their own, have no clear personal educational philosophy and are now lost. A lot of them want the exams returned, but there is no possibility of that."

"Is there anything else we should know?" I asked weakly.

"Well, I can't think of anything else right now. You'll have to see things for yourself.

"Oh, there is one thing," Russell added as we stood up to leave. "Don't be surprised when you lose the trees about halfway."

"Lose the trees?"

"Yes. There was a terrible fire about ten years ago that wiped out the forest in the entire area, hundreds of square miles. I'm afraid it still looks a little bleak."

We shook hands and walked slowly to the car.

Following Russell's directions we found the Port Warford turnoff, which we had been told led to Hoberly Cove over sixty miles of road that Russell had warned us was "not up to Trans-Canada standards." We realized the extent of his understatement almost immediately. About half a mile out of Gander we crossed a single narrow-gauge railway track and plunged into a pothole at least eighteen inches deep. Emerging from that we threaded our way delicately through the enormous light-grey stones that were strewn across our path. We had been told that the highway department was in the midst of paving the first five miles of road. "If this is the part they have worked on," I joked, "I wonder what the rest of it will be like?"

We soon found out. The grey rock stopped suddenly and the road turned into a narrow, deeply pocked track winding through the birches that were held back by sharp ditches cut on each side of the road. We fought our way north, travelling about twenty-five miles an hour and braking continually to soften the impact of particularly deep holes that suddenly opened up in front of us. Each mile took us farther into a wild tangle of spruce, rock and marsh. Jan looked at me, something like terror in her face. "Do you realize that we haven't seen one house since we left Gander? I don't see how we can make this trip more than once in every three or four months."

Just then we entered what the map had indicated would be our first community: Port Warford. Since we knew it had a large elementary school and was the only site of human habitation for twenty-six miles, we were expecting a town of some size. Instead we passed the junction, spotted a gas station and a very few houses scattered along a brown-edged, stagnant-looking inlet, and were still looking for the town when we realized we were through it. Jan looked as if she might cry. God, I thought. We're not on vacation out here. This is where we're going to live.

We were both quiet as we clattered along the road, which to my amazement seemed to be deteriorating. We thundered over a bridge and slowed as we passed exactly twelve houses on stilts. The most remarkable thing about the homes was the front doors, every one of which was at least ten feet off the ground and opened to nothing but air. No steps, no ladder, nothing. This forlorn cluster of houses, seemingly clinging together to resist the marsh that brooded on its east side and the Atlantic that fretted on the west, was Long Arm.

We were nearing the town of Northport when I suddenly noticed something missing. The trees were gone. They had disappeared as if a quilt had been snatched off the land, leaving exposed low rocky outcroppings and the bleached, twisted remains of burned trees. Only young aspens softened the otherwise raw landscape. It was hard to imagine a deader, more forlorn land.

We climbed over a low hill and slipped into Northport. The road stopped at the harbour and all we saw was a row of houses on our left, a clutch of houses and a gas station to our right, and a few dusty goats looking vainly for something green to chew on near a peeling sign that pointed right and read in faded letters: "Hoberly Cove 22 Miles." The only thing in the harbour was the weathered, rotting hull of an ancient schooner lying on its side. The tide was out and the wreck rose out of the shallow water, trailing orange seaweed from its old planks. Bare rock hills rose on the far side of the harbour. Even the bright sunlight could not lighten the feeling of depression.

Outside of Northport the full extent of the fire was apparent. The land was essentially flat, marked by broken ridges and low hills. From the road we could see for miles; only a few green patches marked the spruce groves that had managed to survive the flames. Elsewhere there were only rock and low aspens, their leaves fluttering in the breeze. On our left the rocks and brush tumbled down to a jagged coastline that was bent into coves full of small barren islands. The dust of the road seemed drier without the trees, and it hung in the air, leaving the gaunt trunks and lichen-covered rocks even greyer.

We drove on through this unrelieved desolation, both of us feeling the tension as we drew nearer Hoberly Cove. We turned at a little tavern that seemed ridiculously lost, miles away from any community. In the distance was the blue of the open Atlantic. The sea neared as Rocky Bay inlet opened up before us; we could see the water stretch far along the shore until the land grew hazy on the horizon. Islands dotted the inshore waters, and we glimpsed tiny houses strung along the coast like coloured beads.

"Do you think that's it?" Jan whispered.

"I don't know. It looks pretty small."

At an intersection the hills we had been passing through veered off above us and the land sloped gently for half a mile from the ridge we were on to the water below. I slowed the car and we peered eagerly at the houses spread in front of us. Mostly white with black tarred roofs and coloured trim, they tumbled down the slope to the water, where they clustered densely along the shore. The water was a brilliant turquoise and extended to the curved line separating it from the lighter blue of the sky. The land extended far to the north of us, low, lumpy and dotted with huge rocks and patches of matted spruce shaped by the wind and woven into impenetrably dense thickets often only a few feet high. About a mile away a large purple T-shaped structure squatted in a bog like a huge toad.

"That must be the school," I said. "What else could be that ugly?"

We turned left towards the line of houses, wharves and stages at the bottom of the hill. The first people we encountered were wheeling strange-looking carts along the dusty road: two bicycle tires, it appeared, with a barrel slung between them. As we passed they stopped in their tracks, then followed us down the lane. White picket fences appeared on each side and the straight-sided houses became dense as we neared the main street that ran along the water. With no idea where we were headed, we continued driving wide-eyed through the town. Along our route the townspeople assembled, equally wide-eyed.

"We realized that the road we were on connected with the lane from the high road at the waterfront, then ran north for several miles, linking the communities of Hoberly Cove and Peddle Harbour. Though from the road we could not tell where one began and the other ended except for a small sign welcoming us to one or the other, we found out later that Peddle Harbour was a sandy, house-lined cresent to the north separated from the rocky Cove itself by a small peninsula of land, called Flynn's Point, that held the post office and library. Hoberly Cove was bounded on the south by a curve of rocks and small islands, and from here the road extended another four or five miles to the smaller settlement of Rocky Bay. The three once independent communities now formed the town of Hoberly Cove.

Wondering exactly how to find Carl and May Pike, the people from whom we had arranged through Russell Taylor to rent an apartment, we turned and drove back through the town. Suddenly a pick-up truck sprang up behind, dust flying. It pulled up beside us and the burly, short-haired driver motioned us over, climbed out of the truck, and strode towards me. "You folks must be the new teachers." He extended his hand and smiled warmly. "I'm Hubert Pike, Carl Pike's son. We saw you wandering through town, so I thought I'd catch you and show you our garden. Here, follow me now, back the way you came."

Making a U-turn, we trailed the truck for a quarter mile until it turned into a fenced garden surrounded by five houses, one with an extension I guessed to be our apartment. We pulled up beside the house and got out shakily. The door burst open, and a very short but sturdy grey-haired woman wearing a white apron and printed dress almost exploded from the house. Her face was split by an enormous smile.

"Well, my dears," she said. "You must be exhausted. Come in and have some tea. I'm May Pike and welcome to Hoberly Cove."

2

"Welcome to Hoberly Cove"

The next morning the sunlight woke us as it streamed through the curtainless windows of our new bedroom. As we found out later, our apartment had neither the charms nor the drawbacks of most homes in the community. Containing only two rooms, it nonetheless managed to possess all the essentials, including a bathroom with running hot and cold water—something of a rarity since there was no village water system. Fewer than a third of the homes, we discovered, possessed this luxury.

We woke to piles of pans, dishes, books, clothes and papers: all our worldly possessions (discouragingly valued at $500 when we had crossed the border at Sarnia) heaped throughout the apartment. It was Tuesday morning. I suddenly sat upright, my hands sweating and my stomach cold. Jan, startled, rolled over and looked at me crossly out of one eye. "What's wrong with you?"

"Do you realize," I choked, "that we're supposed to teach tomorrow?"

"Well, that's why we came here, isn't it?" she grumbled. She glanced at the piles of clothes and books on the floor, groaned, and tried to bury her head back in her pillow.

Still in shock, I contemplated my first remarks to my class. "Good morning. My name is Mr. Sawyer"—or should it be "My name is Don Sawyer?" I do want them to know that I am approachable and friendly, but maybe I shouldn't come on too strong. What should I wear? Hell, I don't even know what I'm teaching yet.

I was brought out of my reverie by the sound of the outside door opening and closing, then our own door being tried. I looked out our open bedroom doorway as the front door swung slowly open. A lined, thin red face topped with a shock of grey hair poked into our apartment. Two bright blue eyes danced around the living room, scanned the wall and assessed our bedroom. Jan and I, clad only in our underwear, lay motionless on the bed, staring in panic.

"Well, by jeez. There they are right now, Sophie." A little gnomish man popped through the door and stuck his head into the bedroom. A small potato-shaped woman, her eyes and mouth set in a permanent smile, tiptoed behind him, thrusting her head through the doorway as well.

"Aunty May said not to bother you," he whispered loudly, "but we just couldn't wait to say hello." Jan managed to wriggle into a more modest pose, pulling the covers up over her.

"I'm Enos Pike and this is my wife Sophie."

Enos seemed to feel perfectly at ease in our bedroom with us in our underwear, but Sophie seemed a little more aware of our discomfiture and kept tugging at Enos's arm. Finally, with a last wink at Jan, he turned away. "We'll see you later," he said. "Come up for supper or tea just any time."

"Yes," Sophie agreed, "please do that. We'd be honoured to have you up." She was pulling Enos bodily out of the front door. "We're the upper house in the garden."

As soon as Enos and Sophie left, we heard another knock on our door. May, seemingly indignant that Enos and Sophie had got to us first, made us promise to come to dinner at noon.

"You probably don't like boiled dinner, do you, Mr. Don?"

she asked. The night before she had told us that there were too many Mrs. Pikes around for us to stand on formality with her, but teachers, she clearly felt, were not to be called by their first names, and so "Mr. Don" was her compromise. "Well, I don't really know, May; I don't think I've ever had a boiled dinner. What's in it?"

"You just come over in an hour and see. Carl will be back then, too."

We had met Carl briefly the night before. He had been sitting in a worn chair under a large map of Newfoundland, arms extended on the rests, looking exactly like the mayor of a Newfoundland outport, which, we found out later, he was. His face was red and lumpy, like a piece of weathered rock. His nose was round and slightly off-centre, but his smile and quick blue eyes overrode the severity of his features. The strength of the man was amazing. He easily swallowed my hand in his huge palm and effortlessly crushed it with his short, thick fingers.

Today, as we walked into the kitchen, where the thick crackers and glass bowl of margarine were already sitting on the table, May was bustling around the stove in her cooking uniform: print dress and fresh white apron. Carl walked through the door, almost brushing each side with his powerful, solid frame. It seemed impossible that he was well into his sixties.

"Well, my son, how do you like Hoberly Cove?" he asked. "I suppose it's not much, after what you've come from."

"No, no. On the contrary, we like it—what we've seen of it—because it *is* different from what we're used to."

May smiled as she took the top off a huge cast-iron pot. Carl continued, "Oh yes, everyone here knows everyone else. Not too many years ago, before the road came through, I used to make a run in the large schooner to St. John's for supplies for the whole community. Everyone ordered what they needed and we'd bring it back. If you ran out, why usually people would share what they had. You sure couldn't go to the stores here. If you ran out of supplies in March month when you couldn't get out onto the water or into the woods, you'd find that the sugar which had sold in the fall at fifty cents for ten pounds in the stores here now cost two dollars. And no credit."

May clucked from the stove. "A lot of people died in March month," she said. "If you were sick you had to go by sled all the way to Twillingate over the ice, and that would take two or three days, depending on the weather. Not many made it. Even in summer, it was five or six hours by boat."

"Weren't there any wagon roads?" I asked.

"There were only foot trails," Carl answered, "but you couldn't keep them open in the winter. I remember one time in the spring the ice was still in the harbour here and a woman was coming back from the hospital in St. John's. Eunice Fillier's mother. Well they could only get by boat as far as Warrendale, about sixty miles by trail, and we went up there on foot with a sled. The weather was good and the trail was fairly clear. We didn't have any trouble at all getting to Warrendale, and everything was fine on the way back as far as Thornton. But about seven miles out of Thornton a storm blew up like I've never seen. The snow was so thick your mouth would fill up if you opened it. And cold? My son, it was cold. It was black as coal and we couldn't find the trail. We couldn't go on or back, so we were caught there all that day and night before the storm stopped. It took us almost two days to cover the ten miles between there and Hoberly Cove. We all liked to die before we finally fought our way home.

"Years later, just before the roads came through, they built trails for the large snowmobiles, but before that you just didn't travel much in the winter, and mainly by water in the summer."

May laid plates heaped with bright red meat surrounded by multicoloured vegetables, all exactly the same consistency, before us. To my surprise, it was delicious. Slabs from enormous loaves of homemade bread accompanied the meal. The meat was stringy and slightly salty, but very pleasant. "What kind of beef is this, May?"

"Why, that's pickled beef, Mr. Don. You mean you've never had it before?"

"I guess not. How is it packed?"

"In brine," Carl said. "Now you get it in plastic tubs, but we used to buy it in two-hundred-pound barrels. One barrel would last a family all winter. Salt was the only way we had of preserving

15

meat in those times. We split and salted our fish on the flakes, of course, but there's not much of that any more. Most people around here sell their fish fresh to the plant in Warrendale." The flakes, it turned out, were the dock-like structures, covered with sticks and brown spruce boughs, that were still wedged among the storage sheds along the water.

After dinner we had thin tarts made from marshberries, cranberry-like fruit which grew wild in the bogs that filled the shallow granite basins around the town. May, who had whipped off her apron only long enough to gulp down some dinner and drink a cup of strong tea heavily laced with canned milk and sugar, began clearing off the table, shooing us into the living room. Bravely containing his impulse to bolt back down to his workshop, Carl sat in his chair and finally relaxed.

"What are you building, Carl?" I asked.

"Just finishing off a small boat with Hubert. A little cabin cruiser this time, just for pleasure."

"Have you built many boats?"

"My son," Carl laughed, "I've built more boats than I can remember. I built the largest schooner constructed on this coast. A twenty-eight-ton boat she was, built from timber we cut and skidded in from the woods only a few miles from town. A wonderful boat. I fished on her with my uncles and brother for twenty years off the coast of Labrador. She was the most stable ship on the Labrador. Why, one time my watch broke down in the middle of a roaring storm while we were in the open Atlantic. I took that watch apart, made a new mainspring from some wire and replaced it, right in the worst of the gale.

"I bet I've built or worked on nearly two hundred boats in my time, from schooner to rowboats."

"You said you had plenty of timber to build a schooner. Were there some really large trees before the fire?" Jan asked.

"Timber of the biggest kind," Carl said. "Pine and fir I couldn't put my arms around. Timber that was a joy to work with. The fire was a terrible thing," he added sadly.

"How did it get started?" I asked.

"You'll hear as many stories as people you talk to. But I fought that fire, and talked to the wardens who first found it. They said it was started by a bunch of rich mainland businessmen who were hunting and let their campfire get out of hand. If it had been anyone else, they'd have been tossed in jail for years. But not these fellows.

"I tell you, we almost lost the whole town in that fire," Carl went on. "It was so close we sent all the women and children to Fogo Island. They stayed there for two weeks. The smoke was so thick it was like night for a week. The wind blew the fire up to the high road near Peddle Bay, where we tried to stop it, though we had nothing to really fight it with. There were two or three hundred men with buckets and hand pumps against a fire that surrounded us on nearly every side. The air was so thick we couldn't breathe; some men passed out from inhaling the smoke. Our backs were right up against the sea.

"But the Lord must have intervened, because just as it looked like we were going to lose it—we had boats waiting on the beach to evacuate us, that's how close it was—the wind came off the water and pushed the fire southeast.

"It was a terrible fire. I cried when the smoke cleared and I saw the black trunks of the trees with their green needles burned off. The ponds I grew up with were filled with branches and burned trees. Even the trout died." His voice trailed off.

"The woods are coming back, though," Carl added, his voice brighter. "Last winter you could see thousands of little spruce poking through the snow. In ten years you'll hardly know there'd been a fire, if you didn't know the way it had been."

Carl, who obviously was not used to sitting in one place so long, rose and invited me down to his "store" (a term we discovered was used for any structure that had been or could be used to store anything) to watch him construct his boat. I decided to decline for the moment, as there seemed to be endless tasks ahead of us before our first day in school, and he walked quickly down to his shop set on pilings that ran from the road out into the water.

The next logical step seemed to be to make what preparations we could to begin teaching the next day, so after obtaining directions to the home of Norman Burt, the high school and co-ordinating principal, we drove out of our garden and down the road along the water. The town's harbour began at Flynn Point in the north; the south end of the crescent, which was about two miles long, was formed not by a headland but by a rocky spit and its fragments—several tiny islands and a moss-covered reef called Shag Rocks. Cradled between Flynn Point and Shag Rocks were a dozen boats afloat on the calm blue water. As we passed the spit on the main road we saw that a rutted lane led to an old cemetery covering the peninsula's head, the gravestones silhouetted against the late afternoon sky.

The Burts' home was right on the water in Rocky Bay and somewhat off by itself. It was an unimposing white house with the standard hip roof. A short wing with an extending deck was the only architectural deviation from the basic cube form followed by most of the older homes.

Dora Burt, Norman's wife, answered our knock at the door. When we introduced ourselves she smiled broadly and shrieked from the door, "Norman! It's the Saw-yers. Get off that chester-field and make yourself presentable, now."

She showed us through the hall and into the living room, where a barechested man was lying on the couch on his side, propped up on one elbow. When he sat up I saw that he was a fairly tall man and—except for his distended stomach, which pushed his belt down so low it seemed his pants would fall off—he was not at all overweight. His hair was thinning, and a smile, which completely dominated his face, flickered continually over his features. He looked like a department store Santa Claus off duty.

My first interest was in the books, class assignments and other concerns I thought I should have some familiarity with before 9:00 the next morning. Norman, however, dismissed my inquiries with heaving laughter and a few reassuring words. "Don't worry! Everything will be fine. Just go in and tell them who you are tomorrow; then we'll decide on who's doing what. Would you like to go to the tavern tonight? I thought you'd like to meet Roger and Judy Davies, the other outside teachers here.

18

If you would, I'll call them up and ask them to come too."

Well, I thought, he has been doing this a lot longer than I have. If he says not to worry but to have a beer instead, I'm not going to argue. Jan agreed, so we arranged to meet him at his house later that evening. Then, to relieve Jan's anxieties, we drove to the house of the elementary school principal, Hector Pearce. He was politely glad to see us, but said basically the same thing that Norman had: "We'll worry about school tomorrow."

That night Norman drove us to Chard's, the lonely tavern that we had noticed on the way in to town. Norman explained that there was considerable opposition to the idea of a pub in Hoberly Cove, especially from the Salvation Army. In fact, no alcohol whatsoever, including beer, could be bought in town. If you wanted a beer, there or to go, you had to drive the ten miles to Chard's.

Dora Burt was a soldier in the Army (a member who takes particularly strict vows concerning alcohol, smoking, dancing, etc.) and a staunch opponent of drinking. She was not with us this evening and, from Norman's tone when he spoke about her feelings towards his drinking, I understood that it was a contentious issue between them.

One thing I had noticed in Hoberly Cove was an apparent lack of policing. When I mentioned this absence—a striking one, from an American point of view anyway—Norman told us that the nearest RCMP post was in Warrendale and that constables came through Hoberly Cove only once a week, on Thursday afternoons.

"Well, is there a jail in the federal building?" This situation seemed verging on anarchy.

"Not in the new one. In the old post office we had a jail, but it was only used once in twenty-five years, and that time the prisoner escaped."

"Really?"

"Yeah. A fellow down in Peddle Harbour, who had always been a little cracked, went on a rampage one winter, beat up his wife and started threatening people with a gun. So a few neighbours brought him into the jail and locked him up until he could be shipped out to the mental hospital in St. John's. The first night, he broke out and hid in the bush. Finally he got cold and hungry and came out on his own. Anyway," Norman chuckled, "when we built the new federal building we didn't bother with a jail."

Chard's Tavern was already crowded by the time we got there. It had been located at this remote crossroad, we learned, because it was accessible to Hoberly Cove, Northport and two smaller communities at the end of the other fork: Moresby Cove and Birchy Point. Most of the time these groups got along fairly well, but on occasion community rivalries erupted across the small dance floor. Patrons from Pollardville, a small town near Northport generally held to be populated by madmen, seemed to figure prominently in such disturbances.

The tavern itself was unspectacular. The only decorations on the painted walls were two plastic signs advertising Black Horse and Dominion ales; these hung behind the short bar, where Burt Chard sullenly snapped caps off bottles fished out of a crammed Coca-Cola cooler and drew money across the wet bar top.

While we waited for the Davieses we spoke with Norman about the community. Norman was deeply committed to Hoberly Cove, where he had grown up and lived except for a short stint in Toronto. He was more interested in politics and community development than in education. At least, he seemed to see little role for the schools in solving the problems he outlined.

I was surprised to find out that Hoberly Cove was the last town in the area which still could be termed a fishing village. Most, he told us, no longer had enough gear "to catch a sculpin."

"You see, Don, inshore fishing is dead. The trappers can't even make a living any more. A lot of men go after lobster in the spring, but only a dozen boats fish through the summer.

"Did you see the new community wharf?" We both nodded. We had walked down to the concrete wharf lined with roofed cutting tables the first afternoon and had watched the men in hip boots heave cod onto the cement deck with pitchforks from their bobbing boats tied to the pilings.

"What did you think of it?"

I offered my cautious view. "It seemed pretty nice to me."

"It's completely impractical," Norman said. "It's the only government fishing project we've had in here in the history of the town, and the government built it in a location where sand drifts so heavily you won't be able to dock a rowboat there in five years, much less the long liners we need here. It offers no protection from storms—most boats have to dock in the harbour after unloading—and the facilities are so inadequate that if the number of boats or volume of fish ever increase it will be unusable."

"What do most people who've given up fishing do?" Jan asked.

"Some of them find jobs in Gander, St. John's or Toronto. More are working in Labrador on the Churchill Falls project, but that will end in a couple of years, and what then? We need to develop an economic base in this community before it's too late. We need docking facilities, a breakwater, long liners and a fish plant."

"Do you think you'll get it?" I asked.

"Yes boy. Next year." Norman's earnestness dissolved as his head suddenly tilted towards the ceiling and he hooted with laughter. Abruptly his face snapped back into its former sombreness and his eyes became distracted. "Let me get you another beer," he said, and wandered off towards the bar, grasping men by their shoulders, chuckling and talking as he went.

Before Norman rejoined us, a young couple came through the door. The woman wore wire-rimmed glasses and a knitted black shawl over her slightly stooped shoulders. Her brown hair was pulled back in a bun. Though she seemed to be in her twenties, she looked exactly like my fantasy of a country schoolmarm. The man, who was peering around the room through gold-rimmed glasses, was fairly short and slight, but projected a sense of contained energy. His dark, curly hair had receded prematurely from a high forehead. His face lit up when he spotted us, and the couple walked quickly towards our table. "You must be the Sawyers," he said. "I'm Roger Davies and this is Judy."

Roger and Judy had also followed a circuitous route to Hoberly Cove. Originally from a wealthy suburb near Cleveland, Roger had left the U.S. to avoid the draft, then finished a fifth year of education at the University of Toronto, where he met Judy, who was from Hailleybury, a small town in northern Ontario. Unable to find a job in Ontario, Roger had taken a position the year before in the Hoberly Cove high school and then asked Judy to join him. She did, they were married that winter, and she had taught in the elementary school for the rest of the year. They had bought a house for $600 in the spring, put twice that amount into plumbing and wiring—("We had to wait a month for the electrical inspector to check the work out. The old inspector had been electrocuted and it took a while to find a replacement, I guess.")—and were now living in the house, trying to finish off the interior.

They were evasive about the schools. Roger seemed frustrated, and Judy hinted that she was quitting at the first opportunity. "I tried doing a lot of group work at first, but the idea was so alien the kids didn't know how to respond. Everyone was relieved when I slipped back into a more conventional teaching style, including Norman," Roger told us. Attempts to draw out more information were not very productive. Their hesitancy seemed to be a combination of personal uncertainty and a genuine desire not to prejudice our perceptions. Although they seemed somewhat wary, they also seemed eager to talk, and pleased that we were in town.

"One of the difficulties of living here," Roger said, "is the realization that no matter how long you stay you'll never truly become a part of the culture or the community. You might be accepted as an oddity or as an honorary member, but full acceptance is reserved only for those who are a part of the community from birth."

Norman had finished his rounds and returned to the table, arm in arm with a man—short, red-faced and wearing a blue beret—whom he introduced as Sam Pritchett. Norman was grinning and rubbing his hands together gleefully. "Well boys," he said. "How about stopping in at the house on the way back? Sam here and some of the other boys are coming down and Jack has his accordion. There should be some good times tonight!"

22

We finished our beers and bounced along the road to Norman's in the back of Roger's Land Rover. ("I figured I'd need it—I wasn't sure they had roads here," he laughed. "I was partly right.") When we walked in, the living room was already crowded. Sam was singing a song that approximated the tune being pumped out of an accordion by another man. As he finished, the audience clapped and shouted its approval. Norman nearly bent double, laughing in delight, and we were inexorably drawn into the warmth and excitement.

Norman shouted for a jig and the accordionist began one that immediately had my feet shuffling to the music. A man jumped up and began to hop and stomp with tremendous agility, then one by one the other men and women stood up, their faces glowing, and jigged energetically to the shrieks of the accordion. We were sitting on the couch, enjoying the music but somewhat outside the action, when Sam sprang through the crowd and grabbed Jan by the hand. "Come on, my dear," he grinned, "let's see how you folks jig on the mainland."

The crowd cleared and Jan, seeing that resistance was futile, let herself be yanked onto the floor. Sam began a furious knee-slapping, foot-stomping step while Jan stared, shifting her feet nervously. Then, to my surprise, her heels started clicking and her legs began pumping, arms swaying at her sides. She was tap dancing!

Everyone loved it. They clapped with the tune, admiring her courage if not her step. When the music finally stopped, Sam pounded her on the back. "That was some good, girl," he enthused. "By jeez, stay here for a while and we'll make a Newfoundlander out of you."

"I didn't know you could tap dance," I muttered to her as she fell beside me on the couch.

"Sure," she wheezed. "I took lessons for four years. I always thought it was a grotesque waste of time."

Eventually Norman asked Sam to sing his own songs. Sam gallantly refused until the crowd echoed the demand. Thus persuaded, Sam sang *a capella* one of the wittiest songs I had ever heard. The song told the story of the coming of the Pentecostal

Church to Hoberly Cove, outshouting and out-testifying even the Salvation Army. The song's barbs were personal and droll, yet strangely unmalicious. It included an account of how the United Church had lost its pre-eminence in only a few skirmishes with the Army years before, and now claimed only those who felt that they were so close to God they did not need to shout to be heard. He thus chronicled the history of religion in the town, sparing none.

At midnight we left, anxious about the next day, but the party continued. Reflecting that the evening had seemed like something out of a documentary on Newfoundland, we wondered if all parties were like this one—full of songs and dancing, accordions and spoons, warmth and joy. Or was this a remnant of the past we had stumbled onto by chance?

In two years we never experienced anything like it again.

3

"My name is Mr. Sawyer"

As my first glimpse from the high road had suggested, Squire Memorial Central High School, named for a departed Salvation Army officer, did indeed squat in the marsh like a huge purple toad. It sat on an "island"—a large piece of low, flat granite that barely emerged above the swamp that surrounded it. The building itself was a simple T shape, the rooms lined along a hall with a small gym and auditorium at the east end, severe and unadorned. Even the peeling purple paint and flaking white trim contributed to a sense of gloom.

The building took up nearly every square foot of stable space in its area of the marsh. Since there was absolutely no room for an activities area for either the high school or the elementary school, which was situated half a mile away on the road through town on yet another rock island in the swamp, a floating playground of sorts had been built in between, connected by paths. The entire surface, some five thousand square feet, had been constructed on spruce logs cut, hauled and secured into place by local labour. It was an engineering masterpiece, but unfortunately the job had never been completed. Instead of planting grass on the field or even covering it with sand, the workmen had left it, for ten years, covered with huge, sharp, grey rocks blasted out of a nearby quarry and dumped haphazardly on the corduroy foundation. As a playground, it was virtually useless; it became a parking lot for the teachers' cars.

The obvious question was why, with so much land around the community, they had chosen to build the high school on this rock outcropping in the middle of a swamp. Norman smiled resignedly as he tried to explain.

"When this school was built, Don, the Salvation Army controlled it completely. Now you've no doubt noticed that the citadel"—he pointed at the two-towered white Salvation Army church which formed a triangle with the elementary and high schools—"is right next to the elementary school. When they built the high school, we originally proposed to build it up on the ridge above the high road where there would be plenty of room for expansion. But the Army didn't want it that far away; they wanted to keep an eye on it. Also," and his eyes chuckled, "an important member of the Army happened to own this land." Now he laughed out loud. "And this same man got the construction contract. So here it is."

Wednesday morning, I dropped Jan off at the elementary school. Since we had been in town we had seen very few kids, but now they were swarming like ants between the school and the stores directly across the street, completely disregarding the few cars that tried to worm their way through the throng. Jan was nervous, glancing at the shrieking hordes of kids. I was terrified.

Jan smiled encouragingly, squeezed my hand and waded through the scrambling children seething in front of the elementary school. I had to drive on alone a half-mile farther to the high school. Older kids, high school students, my pupils, lined the narrow one-lane drive. They eyed me with either curiosity or hostility, I was not sure which. As I idled along, travelling barely faster than the walkers, the crowd slowly, unconcernedly flowed around my car, solid in front and in back, and I was surrounded by expressionless faces peering intently into the car. I assumed a look of what I hoped was nonchalance and finally reached the parking lot/playground.

When I opened the battered white main door and stepped into the school, students who had been loudly chattering with each other fell silent as I passed. I could hear them eagerly whispering their impressions in my wake. "He's an American," I heard one say. "Pretty young, I'd say," another offered. "I don't know," replied another," I think he's kind of cute." I glanced at the short, blonde girl with buck teeth who had offered this tasteful assessment and smiled, sending her into paroxysms of giggling.

The inside of the school was as dingy and gloomy as the moors that surrounded it. The building had obviously been constructed on a tight budget. The long, straight, lockerless hall, closed at one end by double doors to the gym and at the other by a door into the office, was lit by only a few light bulbs screwed into sockets in the fibreboard ceiling. The fibreboard was repeated along the walls, the lower section being painted a dark, sombre brown. Together these features made me feel as if I was sealed in a poorly lit sixty-foot mine shaft. The floor was covered with broken dirty tile of some nondescript shade. Not a single splash of colour relieved the dreariness of the corridor.

The staff room/supply room was the first door on my left—a small, nearly cubical room stuffed with books, paper, student desks and teachers. Norman saw me and quickly introduced me to the three teachers I had not yet met. Their faces blurred as I grasped their hands: Willis Collins (seems friendly, nice smile), Alpheus Rowe (oh yeah, he's married to Carl's daughter, I like him), Calvin Sturge (my God, he's big; doesn't look too happy, either). The woman who was teaching French had not arrived yet. Eventually we would have a staff of seven and an enrollment of 165 students.

I talked with Roger for a while, trying to find out what was going on that day. I knew I had been signed up as a history teacher, but Roger seemed as unclear as I was about class assignments. The clock worked its way around to 8:45, then 8:55. I could feel sweat trickling from my armpits down my sides; I was not used to

27

wearing shirt, tie and sports coat. "Roger," I asked, "does everyone wear a tie?"

"Yeah. Last year I created a real furor when I began wearing coloured shirts."

Great. I ran my finger around the tight collar of my shirt. I became acutely aware that I was attired in clothes I had not worn since high school: button-down yellow shirt, an old brown herringbone coat, narrow black pants. Only my shoes were more recent acquisitions. I stared at the bloated wing-tips, bought for my wedding one year ago and worn once, expanding from the ends of my pants like snowshoes.

Finally Norman decided that we might as well get at it. "Well, boys," he said through his wide grin, "what do you say we go in and take attendance, say hello and come back and work out our timetable?" Not waiting for a response, he began dealing out homerooms as though we were playing a game of cards. "Roger, you take nine; Alpheus, how about the sevens? Willis, ten; Calvin, eleven, and Don, you register the eights." What was I supposed to register them with? Where were they, anyway?

"I'll have the bells rung in five minutes. We'll hold them for fifteen minutes, then regroup." It sounded like a military operation. "Here's your registers and registration sheets." I took the papers handed me, had Roger show me where the grade eight homeroom was, and flapped down the hall through milling, curious students.

My room was jammed with old oak desks set in neat rows, the teacher's desk solidly established in the front. Water-streaked curtainless windows, set in crumbling caulking, covered nearly the entire southern wall, looking out on the dismal swamp. The walls were fibreboard painted pastel, a small but substantial improvement over the colour scheme in the hallway, though dun-coloured tile covered the floor with the same scruffy squares. At least the lights, all six of them, were enclosed in glass globes.

I placed my books on the desk and tried to get a grip on myself. Knots of students would form at my door, peek around the edge at me, then run away giggling. When the bell rang, they began to stream into the room, pushing, joking and eyeing me suspiciously. They kept coming until the room was crammed. Still they struggled in. I flipped through the registration papers on my desk. My God, there were thirty-five of them. Eventually it became evident that even the last stragglers had shoved their way into the room. I could not postpone the inevitable any longer.

I was confronted by a sea of expectant, though not eager, faces. They were all looking at me. This was it; I was on. "Good morning," I began. That'll grab 'em. "Uh, my name is Mr. Sawyer."

Compromising, I strode up to the blackboard and wrote in block letters "Mr. Don Sawyer," then smiled ingratiatingly at the people seated before me. They stared back, silent and waiting. Christ, I thought, that's it, gang. I can't juggle and I'm a lousy singer. I experienced a moment of pure, incapacitating panic and felt an inexplicable flash of hatred for Norman. He had lied to me. I knew it wouldn't take care of itself. Now what?

I glanced at my desk and saw the papers huddled on its old, marred surface. I seized them triumphantly.

"OK. Let's get the roll out of the way," I said with relief. I called out the names, each person answering with a flat, mechanical " 'ere."

After I had worked through twelve Pritchetts, four Pearces, three Pikes, four Collinses and a few scattered singles, I reached the Filliers, all eight of them. "Eunice Fillier," I said, giving her last name the French pronunciation. The class erupted in laughter, hooting and slapping each other in their glee. The girl in question hid her crimson face in her hands, giggling uncontrollably. Not sure of the joke, I said, "Eunice?"

"It's Eu-neece," she blurted in embarrassment.

"Oh." Well, geez. It wasn't that funny. "Winston Fillier."

Again the class erupted in hysterics. I was genuinely mystified this time. Finally Winston, a sturdy young man who looked much too old for grade eight (I glanced at his birth date—he was sixteen) looked up and scowled. "That's Fill-lee-er," he corrected loudly. "Not Feel-yay," he muttered under his breath in obvious disgust.

Chastised, I jotted it all down, tried to look official and prayed for the bell.

I had just begun to launch into my life story—were they listening, did they care?—when the bell mercifully ended the ordeal. But even after the halls had filled with noisy, jostling students from other classes, my people continued to sit and stare, fidgeting slightly. Was my life that riveting? No. Well why were they still sitting there?

"Sir," one particularly restless kid near the back of the room finally demanded, "are we excused?" Excused? "Sure. Oh, yeah. Go ahead." The questioner shot me a quick, disgusted look, grabbed his books and streaked out the door, closely followed by the rest of the class.

I sat down heavily in the old wood chair and contemplated my disastrous start. Roger stuck his head in the door and asked cheerily, "How'd it go?"

"Jesus, Roger, it was awful. Those kids looked at me as if they expected me to pull something out of my sleeve."

Roger laughed. "It'll get easier. You know, you were new to them and all. Anyway, can you imagine a less relaxed, more artificial context to try to meet people in?" He was right. Lines of authority, role expectations, past experience, my own tension and everything else had been working to make the classroom cold and strained. "But things will get better," Roger added reassuringly.

"Oh, one other thing," he added. "The eights are regarded as the worst class in school. They ran one teacher right out of here last year. A woman who'd been teaching here for fifteen years. She ended up having a nervous breakdown. The rest of the staff doesn't want anything to do with them, so you may end up having them a lot."

"What's wrong with them?"

"Nothing, really. But they had Maude crying in the staff room half the year because of the things they pulled on her."

"What kinds of things?"

"Oh, they used to ask her why they were memorizing poems." Dangerous radicals, I thought. "And she tried to grab Larry Fillier one time to kick him out and he ran around the class. Maude chased him until she was sobbing. Larry is pretty fast.

There were more things. Ask them sometime."

We picked up our boots, walked back down the now deserted hall to the staff room and sat down at the small student desks wedged into the room. Calvin looked ludicrous as he tried to fold his heavy frame into the narrow space between the chair and the attached desk top. We each were given a floor plan of the school: there were just five classrooms, two bathrooms, a gym, a staff/ storage room, an office, a tiny lab and a smaller library. There were no shop, showers or locker room, art room or home economics facilities. We had no woodworking tools, stoves, art supplies, curtains or lab equipment. The audio-visual equipment consisted of one projector, a broken record player, a bulky reel-to-reel tape recorder without tapes, and a spirit duplicator.

As I studied the floor plan, the process of assigning classes began. I was somewhat surprised that we were undertaking this seemingly rather critical task at this point. After all, I had prepared myself, psychologically and materially, to teach history. ("See," I thought, "it's written right here in my contract.") So why was Norman now asking me if I would like to teach grade eight English? Well, why not? I am really more comfortable with language than history anyway. I agreed.

"And Don, how about English 10?"

"O.K."

"And we've got all this phys. ed. Would you take eight and nine P.E.?"

"Well, uh ... "

"Good. That's girls and boys."

"Then you want some history, eh? How about eight Geography and ten World History?"

Roger looked over at me and grinned.

"Uh, sure."

"Let me see, we've got Math 8. Don, how about that?" This was getting ridiculous. My math is so bad I have a hard time dialing a telephone.

"No math, Norman, for all our sakes."

Alpheaus ended up with Math 8 and I was awarded Art 7 as retribution. What can you do for a year with nothing but manila

31

paper and pencils? I nearly broke out in hives as I looked at my timetable. What was a nice kid from Communication Arts and Asian Studies doing in World History, Geography, Art and Physical Education?

"Roger, you're pretty loaded to be taking on the library this year," Norman said. "Would you handle that, Don?"

I glanced at my timetable. I had two spares in five days. Well, I guessed so. I had always liked books.

"How about sports?" Norman continued. "Who will coach the volleyball teams this year?"

Silence.

"Come on, boys. I'll take the juniors if someone else will take the seniors. Otherwise, we'll have to scratch the team."

He went around from person to person, each giving impressive excuses which seemed fairly convincing to me though Norman would chuckle appreciatively after each story. Norman seemed to find Willis's story—he was working on his house—particularly amusing. "That's true, Norm," Willis added plaintively.

"Yes, boy." Norman laughed. "Sure it is."

Meanwhile I was desperately trying to devise a plausible out for myself. I wasn't sure, but I thought I had played volleyball once or twice in gym during P.E. class in junior high. What twisted fate had landed me in a place that had never seen a football and was surrounded by water that rarely got above 45 ° F., after I had played football for nine years and immersed myself in swimming pools until I had built up a crust of chlorine?

Engrossed in such musing, I was too slow for Norman. "How about it, Don? You're teaching P.E." Now that was a neat trick. After slapping me with teaching P.E., which I had never liked, much less taught, he was using that to qualify me as a coach.

"Well, I don't even know how to play the game," I offered lamely.

Norman sensed a kill. "No problem. The boys on the team will help you out. And so will the rest of us. O.K.?"

"Uh . . . "

"Good. O.K., let's get through the rest of this and go home."

We worked through the morning on timetabling, bus

schedule, duty days and other details that were largely lost on me. I fingered my new red daybook and stared at the neat grid on the first page titled "seating chart." At the bottom of the endless blank pages for lesson plans, to be filled with entries such as: "Chapter 11, page 122, read and do questions at end," were slots marked "Detentions," "Lates" and "Absentees." The back was given to yellow and white sheets labelled "Test Marks." "Grade," "Date and Subject," and "Marks" were the only entries allowed. The whole book was lined off in precise rectangles, defying anyone to tamper with such clarity, efficiency and punctiliousness. The introduction on the inside of the cover explained another feature of the book. "A Personality Chart is provided . . . this is intended to supply an easy means of plotting a behaviour profile. . . . A check mark should be put under a positive or negative characteristic only if that trait is marked in the student above an average degree. Otherwise the check mark would be placed in the centre column under that trait." The teacher who followed this advice was given eleven boxed ranges, including "Practical - Visionary" and "Stable - Emotional." A check was obviously worth a thousand words.

After the meeting broke up, Norman approached me about my English courses. "Russell Taylor, the superintendent in Gander, wants us to try out some new books this year in eight and nine. But I told him it was up to my teachers. So you and Roger can decide."

He took me into the grade eight classroom and showed me a thick book with a torn, faded pink cover that had "Gerald is a lump" scrawled across it. The book was entitled *Adventures in Literature,* and glancing through it I saw that the print was arrayed in tight, black patterns that seemed to say: "If you read this, you will fall asleep." Graphics, in the evident opinion of the editors, would have interfered with the block-like rows of print, and had thus been almost completely omitted except for an occa-sional black-and-white picture of a boy with a fishing pole or of girls in starched dresses and sun hats. Though from all accounts the Hoberly Cove kids had never been more than a few miles out side their community, the cramped stories were set in New York in the 1930s, rural California, suburban America, a dairy farm in Wisconsin. Not even a tale from Toronto. Each selection was followed by a long list of questions. "Boy, this looks like something these kids could really get their teeth into," I commented dryly.

"It was good enough for years," Norman said. "It's literature, isn't it? I mean, the idea is that they learn to read and analyze. Does it matter terribly what they read?"

Could he be serious? "Let's see the other stuff," I said.

"Well, it's not all here. Some of it's novels and creative writing books that haven't arrived yet, but here's what we have."

The new material was still a single hardbacked text, but at least it was bright with engaging graphics. The print was large and the selections more approachable and, to some extent, more relevant, though few of the stories were set in Canada, much less Newfoundland; midwestern U.S. still seemed to hold the edge. At least "Ozymandias" and "Ode To a Grecian Urn" had given way to poetry by poets who were not bound by rhyme and left-hand margins. Some were even alive. I clutched the new book eagerly. "I think I'll go with this stuff, Norman."

"What the hell am I going to do with these?" he nodded at the tattered copies of *Adventures in Literature*.

"You could give them to the Salvation Army," I suggested helpfully.

Carrying copies of my new texts, I wandered across the hall to where the library had been shown on the floor plan. I walked in the door and froze in disbelief.

The room was tiny, only about twelve feet square. Along the back wall were almost bare shelves; a low counter ran under the large, multi-paned window in the north wall. The rest of the room was filled with desks. "We don't really use it as a library," Calvin told me later. "We just don't have enough room. We mostly have to use it as a classroom."

I was aghast. The entire room could not have contained more than 250 books, a fifth of them in two ancient sets of encyclopedias. ("One set was given to us by the Salvation Army Academy in St. John's when they got their new set eight or nine years ago," Norman later explained.) The remaining volumes were largely discards from other Salvation Army schools around the province. They were old, battered and either far too elementary or ridiculously advanced for high school. Virtually all were bound in sombre browns and blues and had been published before 1950. As I glanced briefly at the library's titles, I noticed *The Facts of Life*. I pulled the old, dark blue book from the shelf and glanced at its contents. This was impossible—the entire book was written in German. Was it a joke? An incorrect binding?

I walked back to the staff room, where Norman was checking off textbooks on a large yellow invoice sheet. "Norman, about that library," I began.

"Yes, boy," he grinned. "We got all those books free, we haven't put a nickel into it," he said proudly.

"Well, Norman, I think it's pretty disturbing. How do you expect kids to read when the only book with an interesting title is written in German?"

He looked at me uncertainly for a moment. "Well, it's primarily a place for research." Research?

"But you only have two old encyclopedias in there," I protested.

"Well, these kids don't know how to do a real research paper anyway, so that's all they need just now. Anyway, there's a public library in town." His tone had become defensive, even belligerent.

"Don't you have a budget for the library?"

"I think we get two hundred dollars this year."

"Two hundred dollars a year?" I demanded incredulously. "What have you done with it?"

Norman became more curt. "We haven't had it before. You know, we've only got a decent budget since the Salvation Army relinquished control, just a year ago. We just haven't had enough money to put into library books."

I eased my indignation. "O.K. I can see what you mean, but if I'm in charge of the library this year I'd like to try to build it up so that the kids will have a selection of books that they might enjoy. Can we make sure that the two hundred dollars goes for books this year?"

"I'll look into it," Norman said, and went back to his invoice. I had been dismissed.

I walked to the end of the hall through the double doors into the gym. It had a low ceiling of battered acoustic tile and a floor of the same cheap asphalt tile that covered the rest of the school. It was lit by twelve light bulbs in funnels set in the ceiling. Many of the bulbs were missing or out, plunging part of the gym into a gloom even with the lights on. The floor area seemed quite small (six feet too short for a regulation volleyball court, it turned out), but there was a beautiful built-in stage at the southern end. I walked to the equipment room and unlocked the door with the set of keys Norman had given me along with the P.E. assignment. The room was filled with long folding tables, chairs, broken desks and almost no gym equipment. Besides a single set of uniforms (for volleyball, I guessed, since there were not even hoops in the gym for basketball), there seemed to be exactly two volleyballs—one, deflated—a volleyball net and a badminton net. I knew that there was also a new floor hockey set in the staff room. And that was it. My palms began to sweat again as I thought of teaching P.E. to four groups of kids, two days a week for the entire year, with so little equipment. I considered broaching the subject with Norman, then decided against it.

I closed the door and walked to the SAAB waiting in the rocky playground. As I glanced back at the building, devoid of warmth, materials, facilities, books or direction, I wondered what made it a school. Did learning take place there? Because of it or despite it? Could I change it? Did I have a right to change it? I left more confused than when I had entered.

I drove back through the marsh to the elementary school. Hoberly Academy, as it was officially known, was laid out similarly to the high school, its rooms flanking a single long hall. Like the high school, it was a creaking single-storey frame building, worn and colourless. I peeked into one room and glanced around. There were few materials or books in the room, but a chart hanging on a wall caught my eye. It was a standard alphabet chart with a picture of an apple under A and a boat under B. Under F for flag, in bright red, white and blue, was the American stars and stripes. Though a picture of the queen looked down serenely from the wall, there was not a maple leaf in sight.

Jan was huddled in the staff room with a collection of other teachers. One was droning on in a clipped tone when a short man in thick spectacles cut him off in a strident voice that grated even in the hall. Jan saw me, smiled, and gestured that she would be done in a few minutes.

I walked back down the hall, trying to identify a sharp, pungent odour that pervaded the building. It was clearly coming from the boys' washroom. I decided not to investigate further.

I stood in the front doorway and shivered. The weather was already turning cold, the sea taking on the slate grey cast of the dark sky. A slicing breeze blew steadily off the water, whining between the screen of shops and houses that separated the school from a low peninsula jutting into the Atlantic. A young boy hauled water from one of the public wells and dumped it into a wheeled barrel. In front of me to the left, I could see the federal building containing the library, post office and municipal offices. Two small stores, the Busy Bee (grocery store) and Central Store (dry goods), were in front of me. In a community that had grown in a narrow strip along two miles of coastline, this, such as it was, was the centre of town. I buttoned my coat and went back inside.

The teachers' meeting was just breaking up as I headed back down the hall. The teachers seemed preoccupied with each other, the men arguing and the women talking and laughing among themselves. Finally Jan and Judy emerged from the staff room.

"I told Judy we'd give her a ride to her house," Jan said.

"Oh sure. How did things go?"

We walked down the darkened hall towards the door. "O.K., I guess. I'm teaching first grade."

"First grade? Russell said you were teaching fourth."

"Well, I'm not. There was a lot of confusion and I somehow ended up with grade one."

"Why didn't one of the men take it?"

Judy snorted. "Are you kidding? No man here would be caught dead teaching first grade. I mean, it's just not masculine.

Cecil Parsons says the men have to get them in the upper grades and discipline them before they get to high school."

"By the way, Judy, what smells?" I asked.

"Oh, that," Judy laughed. "That's the toilets."

"I figured that, but why do they smell?"

"Because the school doesn't have running water, and so our toilets are just seats with plastic trash bags under them. The smell is a little ripe in warm weather, but it's not too bad in the winter. Hector, the principal, is supposed to empty them every day."

"Where?"

"In the ocean. He walks down there with them slung over his shoulder and lets the tide carry them away, the same way most of the people in town dispose of their sewage. Have you seen those little sheds at the end of the piers set out above the high tide mark?"

We had; they were scattered throughout the town, but were especially prominent around the harbour in the west end. Most were covered all the way to the water, a drop of ten to twelve feet, and I had wondered what purpose the shafts served. I had thought they were some sort of protected ladder from the water for fishermen.

"Those are outhouses," she continued. "Sewage collects at the bottom and is taken out by the tides." Neat, I thought. "But the harbour gets a little rank, because the water doesn't circulate much there."

We wound through town towards Peddle Harbour, where Judy and Roger lived, past the public wharf and a large garage and store.

The sandy beaches of Peddle Harbour were in sharp contrast to the rocky shores of Hoberly Cove. Judy informed us that people still attached significance to their separate but now indistinguishable communities. "Just above us," she pointed to a low rise, "is Collins Hill, a tight semi-community of its own. And this is our place." She indicated a long drive that dipped from the main road into a low marshy area and ended in an old high-gabled house, newly painted.

We bounced down the rough lane and stopped in front of the

house. "You bought this place for six hundred dollars?" I asked in amazement.

"Yeah, and most of the people around here think we were taken. They said we should have built a little bungalow. Come on in for a minute."

Tired, we agreed to a short visit and ducked through the door in a recently added storm porch. The house was small but warm. A narrow stairway led to the upstairs, where two bedrooms were still being finished. The original construction was as solid as a ship, and thick beams of spruce supported the low ceiling. I unconsciously bent as we entered the kitchen, where the beams were only seven feet above the floor. The kitchen sported new but unfinished cupboards and a dazzling array of matching yellow appliances. A new utility room contained probably the most modern laundry facilities in that part of the island. I thought of Sophie Pike, who still boiled water on top of a wood stove for washing.

On the way home, I asked Jan more about her day. "How is your principal?"

"I'm not really sure," she said. "He did some pretty strange things."

"Like what?"

"Well, he started out by telling me that I had a very bad class"—a bad class? They had only been to kindergarten—"and that I should come down hard on them at first then let up.

"That didn't bother me much, but after I'd just got into class and the kids were still excited and chattering, he walked in the room and screamed 'QUIET!' All the kids shut up as if they'd been slapped. Then he introduced me and said, to the entire class, 'Mrs. Sawyer, there are some real troublemakers in this class!'"

"He said that in front of everyone?"

"Yeah, but that wasn't the worst of it. He went on and said loudly, 'Now you see that boy over there? That's Ralph Whiteway, and that is Alex Pearce. They are bad boys and you will have to keep an eye on them.' Then he glared at the class, said that he still had his strap in his desk, and added 'If any of them give you any trouble, I want you to send them directly to me.'"

"My God. What did you do?"

"I didn't do anything. I was really embarrassed, but I didn't know what to say. I was flabbergasted.

"Anyway, I don't think it bothered the kids too much. As soon as he walked out the door, they all started laughing again."

"How are the other teachers?" I asked.

"I don't know. The women are quiet, except for Judy, and the men seem insensitive to the kids. Everything Hector says Stanley disagrees with, in one tone—a sustained screech. When Hector gets mad he shrills. Mr. Parsons, an old time Salvation Army veteran, argues in a singsong with both of them. The women seem used to it and just sit back and ignore it all.

"One woman seems very nice; Emma Pritchett. She seems to be really good with the kids, but she's teaching kindergarten in the little two-room annex by the United Hall." This was a large decaying community hall across from the United Church. The small school behind it, now used for kindergarten, had once been the United Church school.

Jan seemed drained. We both were silent as we puttered along the fence-lined road. A boy I thought had been in my homeroom that morning was trudging slowly along the side of the lane near our garden. I waved distractedly at him. His eyes lit up and his face split in a huge grin full of white teeth. He waved back excitedly. As we pulled up in front of our apartment, he was still standing, smiling, outside the fence. He waved once more and continued on down the road.

4

"Every man a fisherman, they used to say"

"I don't know if I can make it for a whole year, May." Jan and I were sitting around May's kitchen table on Saturday, sipping tea and munching the accompanying sweet, hard biscuit. We had been teaching for a week and were both exhausted. The year seemed to stretch before us endlessly. "Ten more months," Jan murmured, her voice almost breaking.

"My dear," May said soothingly, "it'll be Christmas before you know it, and by then everyone will know you and you'll know everyone else. Now you just don't worry. Things will be fine. And by spring, if the good Lord spares us, you'll fit right into the schools and you'll feel like you're part of the community."

"Mr. Don," May went on disapprovingly as she looked at the clear tea I was sipping, "that tea looks almost naked." She tittered. "Don't you want some milk?"

I didn't. Mr. Don was far more involved in sorting out the last several confusing days than considering what to put into his tea.

A week in the school and I was already frustrated. Jan loved her kids but found their enthusiasm and energy overwhelming. I

41

didn't know if I loved mine or not, since they sat there silent and distant despite my efforts to reach them through relating scandalous incidents from my personal life-history. What had happened to these kids? Years ago, they had been excited, screaming around the classroom like Jan's first graders, but now their eyes were cold as they followed me around the room. Late-night plotting only contributed to the exhaustion that resulted from my daytime antics.

I was bringing to classroom teaching a set of egalitarian ideals, a broad range of liberal arts courses, the background of two education books, a belief that education should serve the community at large, and a nascent educational philosophy based on the desire to provide my students with a more positive and meaningful school experience than mine had been.

I had attended an excellent high school (ninety-seven per cent of all graduates went on to college) in an excellent community, and hated every minute of it. My most creative moments were spent surreptitiously scribbling poems in the back of the room with one or two other students while the English teacher droned on about *Julius Caesar*. A friend and I wrote a three-act play without our activity being suspected by the teacher, who was talking—for a month—about the metre in *Beowulf.*

My memories of school are of one ordeal after another. I recall Miss Byle covering the board with strange disjointed constructions, straight lines sprouting from other lines like angular trees, that were somehow supposed to teach me sentence structure. I remember studying *Great Expectations* for four months, in every excruciating detail. To this day I hate Charles Dickens. Teachers and counsellors were like trees to me—large, remote and impersonal. I never thought of them as being unsure of themselves, having a family, being loved; certainly they didn't go to the bathroom in the morning. Counsellors were, with one exception, earnest, brush-cut men who constantly rebuked me for not working up to my potential. "See this chart? Well, your I.Q. is way up here but your grades are way down there. You're just not putting out like you should be."

Determined to avoid the crushing insensitivity of my own

experience, I now found myself teaching in a school with an eighty to ninety per cent dropout rate before graduation; a school that saw perhaps one or two from its shrivelled graduating class go to college.

I had not the slightest idea where to begin. In the first week I had discovered that the grade eight English book, improvement that it was, was beyond the reading level of more than a third of my students. The grammar and spelling books were chilling holdovers from another age, and the geography book, called *Southern Lands*, was simple enough, God knows, but so old that many books contained maps of Africa that showed Zaire as the Belgian Congo.

I had spent the first days talking about myself, asking, pleading for questions. Finally one boy in my grade eight class raised his hand.

"Sir," was all I caught for certain. The rest was wrapped around a dialect so thick and clipped that I could only stand looking at him dumbly. "Uh, I didn't quite catch that, Ben."

Benjamin Collins repeated his question, but I was completely lost. My first real substantive question and, after two tries, I was totally unable to decipher what the questioner had said. I opened my mouth helplessly. Ben lowered his eyes and muttered "Aw, nothin'" in embarrassment.

Finally, Warrick Pike, the boy who had eventually asked if they were excused that very first day, eyed me with a mixture of contempt and pity. "He said, sir, does everyone in the States live in big houses and have swimming pools?"

I was more puzzled now than before. "Lord no, Ben. Where did you get an idea like that?"

Ben rattled off an unintelligible reply. I looked beseechingly at Warrick, who sighed in disgust. "He said that everyone on *The Beverly Hillbillies* has a place like that."

As I attempted to explain the economic and social realities of America, I tried to picture the image someone would have of the United States if his primary source of information were the Clampett family, but the concept was simply too bizarre for me to envision.

43

I asked my English 8 and 10 kids to write a short account of their own lives. Not terribly original, I realized, but maybe they were just too shy to talk. What I received was, with very few exceptions, almost frightening. Only one paper was over two paragraphs long and most were only a few short, tortured sentences. One "essay" I received was so full of crossed-out words and doodles that I could hardly make out the text, such as it was: "My name is Eldon Fillier I 15 years old I have livd in Hoberly Cove my ole Live I lik it vere Much."

As I began to see the magnitude of the problem, I approached Norman. "Listen, Norman, there's no way I can work adequately with thirty-five kids, almost half of whom need special materials and special help. We've got to do something about the situation."

"Look at it realistically, Don," Norman replied soothingly. "Half those kids will be gone by Christmas anyway."

"Hell, Norman, that's not much of a solution," I replied angrily.

"Now look," he said. "We're graduating more students now than we ever have before. Why, when I and Harry Rideout graduated fifteen years ago, we were the first graduates in three years. Dr. John Pritchett was the first person to graduate from here, back in the '20s. Why, I'll bet not more than twenty people graduated from here before 1960."

"That's true," Willis added when he saw my surprise. "You see, Don boy, parents just didn't send their kids to school like they do now. I'd guess the average education for an adult in this town is about grade four, wouldn't you, Norm?"

"Probably," Norman agreed. "But they can build boats and houses of the best kind. They can tie nets and fix motors."

From what Norman said, it became clear that school had traditionally been something of a novelty. The curriculum, essentially a slightly modified British curriculum, was absurdly irrelevant in a virtually self-sufficient, isolated fishing community whose economic and social patterns had remained unchanged for hundreds of years, and everyone acknowledged it.

"Anyone who stayed in school beyond grade eight was regarded as something of a freak," Norman said. "You know, the boys on the boats didn't need people who could quote poetry but didn't know a sculpin from a cod fish. And the skills and customs necessary for the life of a fisherman were taught outside of the schools. 'Everyman a fisherman,' they used to say. And so it was, until the inshore fisheries died."

"O.K., Norman, but if, as you say, there isn't much future in fishing, what will happen to the kids who drop out now?"

Norman looked at me uncertainly. "They'll go to work in Toronto or Labrador City, unless we can develop an economic base here. In any case, Don, we can't lower our standards just to put more kids through school." I wondered what sort of standards were worth forcing eighty per cent of a community's young people out of school as failures.

But the fact of social change was excruciatingly evident in the community. Carl Pike told us about having brought in, only fifteen years before, the first gas-powered generator, which had provided six hours of light for a few homes. This was supplanted a few years later by two diesel generators that finally brought electricity to the community as a whole. Roads—however bad—had pushed through the town in the last decade, and daily we saw clouds of dust as tourists rode above the community on the high road.

"When the road first linked us up with Gander," Carl had told us, "this whole part of Newfoundland was jammed with salesmen. They'd come into town, knock on doors and be invited in for tea, as was any stranger. Once in, they'd get people who couldn't read or write to sign for overpriced refrigerators when they didn't have electricity yet. They sold people silverware, three-piece suits, pots and pans, everything. It took years for folks to realize that some people might be trying to cheat them. We'd never seen anyone like that before."

"Yes," May added, "and after them came the antique buyers. They'd pull up to an old house and offer the people a few dollars for a spinning wheel, a chesterfield, a vase, an old brass bed, anything that was old. Well, the people didn't know that these things were worth anything—it was just old furniture to them—so they'd sell for next to nothing. No one will ever know the truck loads of antiques that were taken from this town and sold for ten, twenty, a hundred times what the people here received."

So now Gander was two hours away, Toronto a few days. Los Angeles was even closer, flickering on the TV screens in every home. Glittering visions of New York, Vancouver and California danced nightly on the screens. Children were named after soap opera characters, and plastic chandeliers were hung over the kitchen tables. Incomes, which I was told still averaged only about three thousand dollars per family a year, had been almost uniform across the community for a hundred years. Consequently, a culture had built up based on co-operation and self-reliance. Now incomes varied fifteen thousand dollars from family to family, and the once homogeneous community of fishermen was split into contractors, CN technicians, welfare recipients, diesel mechanics and carpenters. Resentment followed. One man had recently built an addition onto his house with a large picture window that faced the main road. "They put that window there so we can all see their new colour television," Jan and I were told.

But many of the old ways persisted. Horses, used in the winter to haul logs, ran wild along the beach and through town in herds, contemptuous of cars. Fences around gardens were designed to keep the animals out, not in. A sense of trust still pervaded the town, too. When Carl and May left for Gander soon after we had arrived, I noticed that they had left the large skeleton key to the front door in the lock. I ran after them with the key before they cleared the garden.

"You forgot the key, May," I panted.

"Oh, Mr. Don," May laughed. "We always leave the key in the door when we go. That way people will know we're not home and won't bother to stop."

Kindness and generosity had been literally forced down our throats. May had fed us since we had been in Hoberly Cove. She had also taken us down to the Co-op store, a last vestige of the once-powerful fishermen's union, and arranged credit for us. Among the modest shelves of canned goods and boxes were rubber boots, lead cod jiggers (which looked roughly like a skinny fish trying to swallow an enormous double hook), and ashtrays, plates and cups with "Hoberly Cove" stamped on them in gilt letters, some bearing printed pictures of the community wharf and a laden drying flake.

Generally, May would bring us food just as we had walked into our apartment. We would hear a timid knock at the door and Jan would open it to reveal May standing there with a huge plate of fish smothered in scrunchions (chopped and fried salt pork), boiled dinner, or fish and brewis (hard bread soaked in water). "I thought Mr. Don might like a little dinner, my dear," she would say, as though she felt sorry for a man whose wife frittered away her time teaching when she should be home cooking up huge pots of dinner, loaves of bread and endless tarts and pies.

In addition, Nancy—Alpheaus Rowe's wife and Carl Pike's daughter—had brought us potatoes, carrots, cookies, and a bookcase, and had offered us the use of her freezer. Enos and Sophie had brought us a gallon of the wild blueberries that grew everywhere in the marshes and burned-over flats. Carl took me to the community wharf and bought us a six-pound cod for twenty-five cents. While there, we stood by the cleaning tables and watched the few boats still fishing unload and clean their fish. A quick slash, a tug, and the orange liver and dark entrails lay glistening on the table, to be washed into the shallow water for the waiting gulls, huge flounders and green crabs that glided around the pilings. But I noticed that only cod poured from the open boats by the wharf.

"Don't they catch anything besides cod, Carl?"

"Oh yes, mackerel, thousands of flat fish, bloody crabs by the buckets." As if to prove his point, a king crab twelve inches across its spindly legs flopped onto the dock.

"Why don't they keep the crab?"

"No market. The fish plant takes nothing but cod."

"What do you do with the mackerel?" I asked, thinking of the boxed salt mackerel I had relished as a kid. "Does anyone salt it?"

"Clyde Tippett down in Rocky Bay still puts some up. Old Clyde's one of the few, though. He's quite a fellow," Carl chuckled. "He still makes snowshoes from birch, one of the last around here. He runs traplines in the winter, too. Most fellows catch only the odd mackerel in the gill nets because the mesh is too big, but the cod-trappers get plenty of mackerel. I dare say you can get as much of it as you like."

A fisherman whittling the tongue out of a large cod looked at us briefly. "If it's mackerel you want, I'll bring you some in," he said, his back to me. "Paul's in your class, I believe. I'll tell him when I have some." He then offered me a plastic container full of cod tongues, which looked somewhat like raw oysters. I was at a loss, but Carl assured me that they were delicious and that May would cook them for us, so I accepted them gratefully.

The next day was Sunday. The morning was warm and sunny so Jan and I drove a short way out of town and walked up into the tangle of bushes above the road, buckets in our hands, to pick blueberries. Though we returned blue-mouthed in the after-noon, laden with huge, juicy blueberries, I was still craving the mackerel Carl had mentioned. I got directions from him to Clyde Tippett's and drove through town towards Rocky Bay. I parked the car in front of the modest house and walked around to the back, since the front door was some three feet over my head with-out a stairway. A teenaged boy was chopping wood near a shed. When I told him who I was and what I wanted, he dashed into the house and brought back with him a wiry older man with soft eyes. I introduced myself and shook his hand.

"You're the new teacher in the high school, sir?" he asked.

I squirmed uncomfortably—this man was three times my age. "Yes, sir."

"Well, I don't have any boys left down there. Jesse there," he nodded towards the boy still chopping sluggishly at the chunks of wood on the ground, "left school last year in grade eight. I told him he should go on, but he wouldn't listen to me." Jesse never even looked up.

When I mentioned that Carl had told me he cured mackerel, Clyde's face lit up and he nodded emphatically.

"No better fish in the sea for my taste. I like it almost as well as salmon. Most folks say they don't like it around here, but I'll bet four-fifths of them have never tried it. You stay right here and

I'll get you some." With that he bounded excitedly into the house.

Jesse stopped chopping. "You hunt?"

"A little," I said. Well, I had hunted once or twice. Never got anything, but tried.

"I run rabbit snares in the winter," he said. "And last year I got a moose." He left his axe in a log and moved towards the shed. Suddenly he reached into the shed, grabbed a pitchfork and began to stab frantically at something wriggling in the weeds. I stared at the boy jabbing savagely at the tall grass and tried to imagine what he was attacking with such fury. I knew there were no snakes on the island, and the faint mewing I heard could not have belonged to a rat. Satisfied, Jesse tossed the animal into the air with a look of triumph on his face. A tiny kitten flew off the tines of the fork, tumbled limply in the air and fell into the field a few yards away.

I felt nauseated. Jesse looked at me, still smiling, then saw the shock and disbelief in my face. His own face fell back into a sullen mask.

"My God," I finally stammered. "Why did you do that?"

"It's just a kitten. It'll grow up to be a cat. I hate cats. I kill every one I find. Last winter I killed more than twenty. All they do," he sulked, "is piss on the snow and make it dirty."

The entire episode had been so grotesque and unexpected that I was not yet able to fully comprehend what had taken place. Before I could react further, Jesse's father returned, beaming and clutching a large bag.

"Here you are, my son," he said cheerfully. I looked numbly into the bag, which held four dried mackerel and three split cod.

"I killed another one of them kittens, Pa," Jesse said from the shadows of the shed.

"That's shocking, boy, just shocking," Clyde responded without much conviction. He looked at me and shrugged. "I tell the boys they shouldn't kill these cats, but I guess the place would be crawling with them if they didn't, eh Mr. Sawyer?"

"How much do I owe you for the fish, Mr. Tippett?" I managed to ask, anxious to get away.

"Not a thing, not one penny sir," he smiled warmly. "And if you ever want any more, just stop in and you'll have as much as you like. And we'd be some pleased if you'd stop by for tea or supper some evening."

I thanked him and climbed back in the car, still shaken. I was as confused and horrified by Clyde's apparent acceptance of his son's action as by the act itself.

I had just got back home and placed my hand on our door knob when the Pikes' door swung open and May emerged into the porch. She slammed her door shut behind her and walked by me, her face averted. "Hi, May," I said.

She never even looked at me. "Mr. Don," she acknowledged brusquely, then strode through the outer door, shutting it with a bang. Perplexed, I walked into our living room, where Jan was working at the table.

"What's wrong with May?" I asked.

"Do you think she's acting funny, too? She's ignored me all day. I thought maybe it was just me."

Roger and Judy stopped over that night and, since they had lived in our apartment most of the previous year, we asked them why they thought May would be treating us so coolly. Judy laughed knowingly. "You picked blueberries today, didn't you?"

"Well, yeah."

"That's it," she explained. "Today's Sunday."

"Yeah, so what?"

"You're not supposed to do anything on Sunday, at least not in this house."

"You mean," Jan asked, "that she's upset with us because we spent a few hours in the woods picking berries?"

"You've got it," Roger said. "Sunday is supposed to be a day of rest, and they're not kidding. Last year we used to go into Gander every weekend so we could enjoy our Sundays. Since we moved into our own place, we just don't worry about it much."

"So what are you supposed to do?"

"You're supposed to sit at home, read the Bible, and go to church in the morning and again in the evening. If you don't,

50

you either do what you like and don't worry about what people say, or you don't let people see you up and around."

"Was there a lot of pressure on you to go to church?" I asked. We had already been emphatically invited to the United Church, the church of the social and economic elite, by the Pikes. We had managed to demur once, but the issue was far from dead. "I hate to hide behind being a Baptist to avoid attending," I said.

"There was a lot of it at first," Roger said, "but remember, we were the only real outsiders who'd lived here for years, so we faced more pressure than I think you will. We refused to go, and the rumour got around that I was Jewish, then that we were Mennonites. Things got really weird when the Pentecostal minister came into my room after school and accused me of teaching evolution in science class."

"What! I thought the Scopes trial settled that issue forty-five years ago."

"Maybe in Tennessee, but not here."

"What did he say?"

"He just said I had to stop teaching lies that were contrary to the story of creation as found in the Bible."

"Didn't Norman back you up?"

"Back me up? Hell, believe it or not most of the staff agreed. Calvin doesn't believe in evolution now. Norman told me that if I was going to teach evolution I had to give equal time to the biblical interpretation. And that I had to be impartial while doing it."

"What did you do?"

"I stopped teaching the theory of evolution."

Most Sundays we drove out to Salt Pond, a small shallow lagoon a couple of miles east of town that was separated from the sea by a sand bar. To the north the pond lay against a line of dunes that fell to the ocean in a broad, flat, sandy beach which stretched for several miles. We would walk for miles along the sand, peering at the strange sea creatures and hundreds of lost lobster pots that littered the beach. Though reportedly one of the finest beaches in all of Newfoundland, it was generally deserted, especially as the fall wore on. Usually we would go alone, but sometimes Roger and Judy or Doreen Wyatt, the French teacher, would accompany us.

Doreen was from an old Ottawa family and told us facetiously that she had come to Newfoundland seeking Canada's noble savages and the breeding grounds of her beloved Newfoundland dog. Instead, she had found herself alone, isolated in a small village of unemployed fishermen, and removed from the friends and refinement of Ottawa. She also found that Newfoundland, while indeed the ancestral home of her dog, was almost devoid of the huge black beasts with webbed feet.

"What happened to them?" I asked.

"The breeder in St. John's told me the dogs completely died out in Newfoundland; the breed was maintained in Europe. He said their downfall was that they were quite tasty. Fishermen used to take them on their schooners, especially when they'd go for months up the Labrador coast, as a mascot. They were strong swimmers, of course, and saved many fishermen washed overboard."

"But," she was almost in tears, "when things got tough and provisions ran low, they'd kill and eat the dogs."

Doreen had found it hard to believe that students who had supposedly been exposed to French for three or four years could not ask, "How are you?" The students, on the other hand, could not believe that anyone would expect them to. After all, they had never been taught French before by anyone who spoke the language.

As for me, as I began my second week of teaching it became absolutely apparent that I was not going to be able to rely very much on that new English 8 literature book. Because of its reading level, and also because the kids were intimidated by anything that had a hard cover and was handed out by an English teacher, the book was simply not going to work.

I began to search for some alternative to the process of assigned reading, dreary "discussion" (usually a teacher's monologue) and homework questions—a process that had dominated English for most of these kids and had turned many of them away from reading. What it had really taught them was that they could not

52

be successful in any case. And they were also convinced that English could be no other way. The idea of English as having something to do with communication—alive, verbal and stemming from their own experience—was as alien as nuclear physics. Spelling had been the systematic memorization of strange words which they had never seen and would probably never use again. Grammar was the study of gerunds, conjunctions and subordinate clauses: a system of technical, abstract rules they had "had" for a minimum of nine years—and yet most of them were unsure of tense and number agreement, had no idea where to stop a written sentence, and were not even clear on what periods were and where they went. Double negatives abounded in their writing and capital letters were interspersed randomly throughout; they knew they were supposed to be in there somewhere. More pathetically, my students were afraid to write: they had been slammed so many times for their mistakes that they had lost a desire to correct them; now, they only wanted to avoid them.

Besides books, one of the things Jan and I had brought along to Hoberly Cove was a box full of my favourite Marvel comics: *Spiderman, Thor, The Fantastic Four, The X-Men, Dr. Strange* and *The Hulk*. They were bright, exciting and inviting, and the plots were not entirely devoid of literary and philosophical content. I had read them avidly in college and now I decided to use them to prove that, at the very least, English was going to be a little different this year.

The first few days I just dumped them on the class, asking the kids to simply read and enjoy them. Then we talked about the characters—their personalities, physical characteristics, uniqueness, etc.—and how the writers had developed the characters in their stories. So when I asked the students to dream up their own super-heroes and write a character sketch on them, complete with portrait, there was hardly a murmur of protest. Some kids were terrified at having to tax their imaginations in school, but the idea was engaging enough to override most hesitancy. After that, character sketches for their own super-villains were a snap, and the final assignment, a story, grew naturally from inherent conflicts between the characters they had developed in their sketches.

The results were the first evidence of the brilliance and imaginativeness of which these kids were capable. Tiger Lady, the Red Hood, Saturn Man and the Iron Mask battled it out in stories that raged across galaxies, many profusely illustrated. Warrick Pike, who was as slight as his good guy, Supper Hero (spelling was not his strong point), detailed how his hero's muscles were "too small to be seen, but he can lift up a steam shovel with one hand." Warrick pitted his hero against Magness, "a mad creature from a lost planet in space who left it to terrorize the living creatures of this solar system," who wore "razzor toes on his boots." The epic encounter between Magness and Supper Hero was called "The Last Battel."

The Last Battel

It was early monday morning and New York city was in Terror, the police and the Mayor were showered with phone-calls about a Sacer shaped U.F.O. in the sky above the city. In the west end it had burnt a huge bulding to cenders.

The Mayor was answering a phone-call when a large creature, apered and placed a scroal in his diske and disapered again.

The mayor picked it up and read it.

It demanded that Supper Hero be shut and his body turned over to Magness or he would destory the city.

The mayor pressed the red bottom that set of the allarm in Supper Heros hide out. Supper hero opened the hide-out doors and shut out trough, in a few minets he was in the mayors ofice.

The mayor imeadly explended to him the sititeon. Supper Heor shake his head and shert out the window and upward.

at two thousand feet he had a clear view of the space ship. He new that befor the villen could be brought to justice, that ship had to be destraed. He went up to about 200 yads. from the space ship and fired a full force lazzer beam at it. It did no good and the ship rebeled it with a blast of energy ray witch bearly misted him. Since thi failed he shot both of his rays at it at the same time but it was in vane. the ship shot buck with

54

another ray witch missed him by lest then a inch. Then the ship disappered in the distance.

The tale went on for four pages to detail more encounters fought in the wilds of the "Andy's Mountains."

The story was obviously imaginative and reflected a great deal of thought, but what was I supposed to do about Warrick's horrendous spelling? Thus far I had been primarily interested in getting the kids to write enough to work with, so I had been only encouraging in my comments, avoiding red slashes and laying on instead heavy praise for flashes of creativity or even sincere efforts. But now I was confronted with a paper (actually, several fit into this category) by a talented, creative writer who desperately needed assistance in the mechanics of English. Nine years of spelling drills had clearly not been the answer.

After several days of agonizing, I called Warrick in. I had written a comment on the paper praising it for its originality but studiously avoiding any mention of mechanics other than to note that some of his words had been a real challenge to decipher. Well, I decided, I would confront him with the problem and see how he felt about it.

"Warrick, I read your story and I really enjoyed it."

"You did, eh?"

"Yeah, but Warrick, some of your words were a little hard to figure out."

"I know," he lamented. "I can't spell worth nothing. Never have been able to. Old Maude used to refuse to take my papers, the spelling was so bad."

"Well, it's not that bad," I lied. "You just tend to spell words like they sound, a real disaster when you're dealing with English. Also, you're using words you've heard but probably never seen written, so naturally you're going to have problems. Anyway, I didn't want to dampen your enthusiasm by correcting them all; I know that that can be pretty demoralizing. So I wanted to ask you what you wanted me to do about corrections, and how we could work on your spelling generally."

Warrick looked at me strangely. "The only way I'll ever learn it, I guess, is if you make the corrections. Go ahead and do it."

"All right, but what I'll do is put the correct spelling above your word so you can compare them, figure out patterns, see your mistake and maybe remember the correct spelling next time. O.K.?"

Warrick nodded his head gravely. In the next two years we made lists of his misspelled words, put them on flash cards, reviewed rules and tried every other device I could think of. But though he improved, Warrick still can't spell worth a damn.

Spelling was the issue that Norman and I first clashed over, too. One afternoon he called me into his office after classes. "Don," he said, "Sterling Fillier's mother called up and told me Sterling hasn't brought his spelling book home yet this year. She says Sterling isn't a good speller and needs to work in his book."

"I'll certainly agree that Sterling isn't a good speller, Norm," I said, as I rummaged through my papers trying to find his latest effort. Sterling was one of only a few kids who were still hesitant about writing. He had no confidence in himself and looked at the floor shyly, remaining dead silent, if I tried to talk to him about the situation. "Look at this paper." It was the super-hero story most of the kids had enjoyed. Sterling's entire effort was about eight lines, which was not bad for Sterling. "Do you see the words he's misspelled? 'Off,' 'too,' 'spike,' 'said,' 'listen,' 'know.'"

"Well, that proves her point. You should be spending more time working on spelling."

"I am working on spelling, Norman; I'm just not doing it out of the book." I leafed through the grade eight speller lying on his desk. "Do you know the words we would be working on this week?"

"No."

"Sabotage, mortgage, pacify. This isn't going to help Sterling. This is the sort of stuff he's had all his life—words that are alien to him, just sounds. They're not part of his vocabulary. There is just no link between Sterling's world, his vocabulary and the twenty or so words he's been arbitrarily assigned every week for the past nine years."

"Don," Norman smiled, "do what you think is right. But how about sending the book home? And something else. You can't prove the success of a new approach by comparing it to the failures of the old. You have to prove success on your approach's own merits."

I never sent Sterling's spelling book home, but in the months to come I did think a lot about Norman's last remark.

Meanwhile, the situation in my geography classes was even worse than that in English. The geography text was one of those old books with large type, black-and-white pictures of gauchos and Mt. Kilimanjaro, and lists of national exports. In the back of each chapter, under the heading "Questions," were columns of queries designed to really bring the study of cultural geography alive: "What is the highest mountain in Chile?" " The largest city in New South Wales is_____." "Name three major products of Peru."

"Well, folks, where do you want to start in geography?" I had asked as the kids leafed forlornly through their books. No one answered.

"O.K. then, what did you study last year?"

"Uh, we studied Canada," offered one boy.

"We did not," a girl said emphatically. "We studied America. We studied Canada the year before."

"Yeah," agreed Roland Fillier. "And the year before that, and the year before that."

"O.K., then. A little quiz. How many provinces are there in Canada?"

"Five?" asked one girl.

"Seven?" someone tried.

"Twelve?"

"No, ten." This was worse than I had expected. "O.K., what are the three major parties in Canada?"

"Parties?"

"Yeah. You know, political parties."

"The Liberals." Randy Whiteway said.

"Good. What are the other two?"

"The Democrats?"

Anything had to be an improvement. The curriculum guide stated that we were to spend nine weeks on Australia, nine weeks on South America, nine weeks on Africa, and the remaining nine weeks on the geography and geology of Newfoundland. At this point in my teaching career, I still felt obligated to at least nominally follow such dictates.

"Listen, how about starting with Africa?" I suggested. Sure, why not? We could start with Albania as far as most of them were concerned. "But let's get a few things straight first. What do we study when we look at geography?"

"Land, rivers, mountains."

"Yeah. What else?"

"Climate."

"O.K. Is that all?" Silence. "What about people?" They weren't too sure. "Look, everything you've named is important because they affect people. So this year we're going to look at geography not only as a study of a country's physical features but as a study of the country's people as well. This is because people, in order to survive, must adapt to their environment. That's why we look and act and live differently. You know what I mean by environment?" They didn't. "Well, that's everything around us, our surroundings. For example, how has the environment of Newfoundland shaped the way people live here?"

From there we launched into a discussion of fishing, hunting and hauling firewood that somehow ended up with Warrick talking about how cold it could get in the winters.

"I've woken up some mornings before the stove's been lit—the floor's some vicious cold—and I've had to break the ice in the wash basin before I could wash my face. That's true, sir." Silent nods around the class left little doubt that it was.

I ran off lists of the forty African countries with their capitals and population, grossly different from the information in our texts, and handed them out. "What do you say we each pick a country, do some research on it and report to the rest of the class?"

This sounded safe enough. "O.K., then, how can we get information on our countries?"

In unison: "Encyclopedias!"

"Ah, but some of your countries aren't even in our encyclopedias. And anyway, you can't use them."

"What? Why not?"

"Because I want you to think about where else we can go for information."

Books and *National Geographic*, the one magazine received by the school, was about all I could elicit. "How about films?" Oh, yeah. "O.K., I'll bring in the National Film Board and Department of Education catalogues, and you can pick out some films. But come on, if you wanted to know how your aunt in Toronto was getting along, how would you find out?"

"Call?" Maybe rhetorical questions weren't a very effective teaching technique.

"O.K., but you could also write, right? Well, let's write these countries and ask them for some information."

"You mean, write Africa?"

"We don't even know the address!"

We figured out the addresses, and the form of the letter, and that day we wrote letters to Africa, in English class. Maybe it was at this point that the distinctions between my classes started to blur. At any rate, the next day thirty-five letters were winging their way from Hoberly Cove to the dark continent, some even painstakingly pecked out on the school's single typewriter, which I had borrowed from the office.

Three or four weeks later, the information began to pour in. When the first student got his thick brown package from Kenya, he called me excitedly at home. Each day someone received an envelope with exotic stamps; we gathered around as he showed the rest of us what he had received. Two packets were greeted with particular enthusiasm. The first, from Cameroon, was a beautifully illustrated hardbound book, some three hundred pages in both French and English, the country's two official languages. And from the Republic of the Congo we received, along with other material, a gorgeous full-colour portrait of its president, Manien N'gouabi, in a military uniform heavy with braid and encrusted with medals and decorations. We all decided that he cut a dashing figure and that since we didn't have the queen's portrait, he should occupy the monarch's position of distinction in our room. Without a doubt we were the only classroom in Canada to have Mr. N'gouabi staring benevolently from high on the front wall.

It was my History 10 class, at this time, that was forcing me towards drastic innovation. Though fewer in number, the grade tens, whom I also taught English, proved far more frustrating than my other classes. As we moved into October and my classes began to take on personality, my grade eights, who had seemed so difficult that first day, were quickly becoming my favourites. But the grade tens still seemed monumentally indifferent. Essentially, I received no student response whatever, and my fragile concept of inductive teaching was in a shambles. Whenever anyone would show some interest in what I was doing, the others would ride him unmercifully. They were extremely immature, I decided.

My approach to history had been very different from the way I tackled English. I had spent forty-six credit hours in college mulling over obscure books on the intricacies of modern Chinese history, had perused microfilmed copies of the 1927 *Shanghai Courier,* had researched numerous erudite papers, and had generally followed a methodical, time-proven pattern: read, discuss, regurgitate. Being highly motivated, I had mastered a great deal of material, most of which I was now rapidly forgetting. Nonetheless I began teaching history with confidence that my methods and my enthusiasm would produce a roomful of dedicated historians. Unfortunately, or fortunately, my students did not care "Why each of the four ancient civilizations we studied grew up along rivers," a question I featured prominently on my first quiz, this idea having been a major theme in my coverage of the subject.

I could not understand it. I had distributed copious notes and supplemented our boring but adequate text with other material that I had brought for that select purpose; I had even tried to throw in some sex and humour. We had covered every page, every concept in detail. Yet when I gave the first quiz—five obvious, open-ended questions—two out of twenty passed. And wrong answers were not usually the problem; in most cases there was simply no attempt at all. I received test after test with one feeble answer and three or four blanks. The only feedback that I got was one comment from Sarah Collins, one of the two students who had passed. "Well, sir," she said acidly after I had ranted at the class for a half a period, "we're not used to answering questions where we have to think."

Undaunted, I pressed on. In specifying the chapters to be covered, the curriculum guide predictably omitted sections on non-western culture, specifically China and India. I was not buying that, of course, since half my personal library concentrated on these very areas. Ah, I thought, I'll really wow them. I'll make Chinese philosophy come alive. We'll spend endless hours discussing the Taoist concept of non-action, the interdependence and interaction of yin and yang in a harmonious whole, the principles of Confucianism.

I prepared, typed on stencils and ran off a twenty-page summary, single-spaced on long paper, of Chinese philosophy during the Classical Age. It was a masterpiece of condensation, and represented a week of working until one or two in the morning. Never mind, I thought as I swilled coffee and worked on into the night, when I spring it on them in class it will all be worth it.

My efforts were met with a collective yawn. All my work aroused only casual interest on the part of a single student (who told me later he only acted attentive because, being the ace history student, he knew it was what I wanted). And the final unit test on the whole section, many of the questions being identical to those on the previous quiz, was a disaster. In fact, the results were even worse. Questions like "What are some of the general characteristics of Chinese philosophy?" and "Explain the meaning of the story of Chuang Tzu and the tortoise" (one of my favourites) were left blank on paper after paper. It broke my heart.

It was not until a week or so later, still plodding along in the book, that I finally recognized the real problem. We were talking about ancient Israel when Paul Pritchett, my star pupil (at least he had known who Lao Tzu was), said, "Aren't they fighting over there now?"

"Yeah. They sure are." Was he joking?

61

"Why?"

"Well, there are a lot of reasons," I said, relishing the opportunity to launch into a long discussion on the intricacies of the Palestinian question. "I guess the root of the problem lies in a religious conflict that's hundreds of years old. You all know the main religion of Israel, of course." Twenty blank looks. "Don't you?"

Dead silence. "O.K., Paul. What's the main religion of Israel?"

"I'm not sure. Are they Christians?"

In a class of twenty grade ten students, not one knew the primary religion of Israel, much less of the surrounding Arab countries. We had been spending a month and a half on the political shifts of ancient Mesopotamia while one of the major trouble spots of the world was a total mystery. I went through the routine I had tried with my eights. Everyone knew what party was in power in Newfoundland, but only half of the class was sure which party was in power nationally. No one knew both major opposition parties, and everyone thought that the prime minister was elected by direct national vote.

From this point on, our class began to change. The kids had asked me repeatedly why we were studying "this old stuff," and suddenly I had run out of adequate explanations. I talked the situation over with the students, and they all agreed that they were fed up with the textbook. "But what can we do? I wish we could throw it out the window," Violet Parsons grumbled.

"Well, we can, if we can devise a better way to spend our time."

They stared at me in disbelief. I walked over to the windows and, with a fine flourish, threw my book through the open window near the ceiling. The book sailed through the window and slapped on the rocks outside.

The class gasped. Suddenly I realized that they were preparing to launch their books as well.

"Hold it!" I yelled. "That was only a symbolic gesture. There's nothing wrong with this book, it's just how we use it. See." I grabbed another one and flicked to the section covering the establishment of Israel in 1947. David Ben-Gurion looked up at me sternly. "Here's an explanation of the whole Israel question. Let's look at it, and then talk more about what we want to do with our time for the rest of the year."

The final form of our history class did not take shape for several more weeks, but for the time being I began to record the CBC local and national news twice a week. Since virtually none of the kids listened to the news or (since none were available) read newspapers, I played the recording in class and we discussed the main points. This was the start of a process that turned our history class into a study of the social realities of the world, the country, the community and perhaps most significantly, the school, and how these realities affected our lives. Only one person really objected. "What if we get on *Reach For the Top?*" she asked seriously. "We won't know the answers."

The form remained fluid, and at this point we had barely begun, but our direction was clear.

5

"If they don't make it, that's their fault"

Our SAAB was a big hit from the start. Its unusual shape and the buzzing produced by its two-cycle engine had made it the greatest curiosity on four wheels ever to appear in Hoberly Cove. Men I had never met would walk up to me in a store, nod, then ask, "Does that little car really only have three cylinders?" I would smile and assure him that it did. "And you really have to add the oil to the gas?" Again I would nod, at which he would laugh out loud and walk away shaking his head. Some people, however, apparently looked upon the car less as a novelty and more as an embarrassment.

Shortly after we had arrived in town, the same erratic running that had plagued us on our trip to Newfoundland returned to haunt us. Sometimes I wondered if the car was not simply retaliating for being left out in the bitter cold. One day as I tugged at wires and swore at the little engine, Carl walked up and studied the car for a few moments in silence. His eyes noted the rust that had broken out along the bottom of the doors; the smashed tail light lens I had tried to epoxy together, a piece of red cellophane making up for a few missing pieces; the various dents and scratches I had tried to cover with paint that never matched; the splotches of red emerging from the flaking blue paint I had applied to a fender cannibalized from another car when ours had been crumpled against a post.

Finally he turned to me and said, "I suppose you'll be buying a new car soon? A bigger car most likely."

I looked up. "I wasn't planning on it," I said. "Why?"

"Well, it's just that what with you and your wife teaching you should be bringing in plenty of money"—Jan was making under four thousand dollars for the year's work and I was making around five—"and, well, I'd think you, being a teacher and all, would want something a little more, uh, dignified."

I assured him I had no plans to replace the car.

I had already found out from Norman that Morgan Pearce was probably the best mechanic in town, so when the car finally refused to start one morning, I had Carl tow me up the hill and unhitch me by the closed double white doors to the small garage. I noticed that only the front of the building was painted and that the windows of a small store-front structure attached to it were smashed. I knocked on the doors, waited, and finally heard someone lifting a beam on the inside. The doors swung open slowly, revealing a murky interior lit by what little light managed to filter through a single filthy window, supplemented by a lone light bulb hovering over a workbench heaped with wires, rusty wrenches, empty oil cans and beer bottles.

In fact, as my eyes became accustomed to the gloom, I saw that dozens of beer bottles studded the cramped interior. Dominating the building was a car parked on the wooden floor. Along one wall, sitting on a log, a wheel and the floor itself, were three men, all swigging intermittently at bottles of Dominion ale. A beer case, still half full, lay precariously atop the litter on the workbench.

As I walked in each man nodded at me solemnly. "Morgan Pearce?" I asked.

"Yes, boy." The voice seemed to come from beneath the floor. As the three men continued to stare at me silently, I squatted down and looked under the car. The grease-encrusted floor was cut by a three-foot-wide space that extended about ten feet in length. Through this hole I looked into a dark, nightmarish cavern. The wooden floor I was standing on was propped up by unpeeled poles, which were imbedded in the crater dug out below. Oil cans, crusty exhaust pipes, old shock absorbers and various other decaying car parts lay partially buried in the oily slime that covered the bottom of the pit. Sloshing around below was a man in green overalls, his grimy face illuminated by a trouble light, its cord twisted and taped, hanging from the front of the car. Despite the grease and grime smeared on his face, his complexion seemed deathly white in the stark glow of the light. His big eyes swivelled from the wrench he was tugging on and looked at me.

"How do you do, sir." He smiled broadly, showing large white teeth. "You're Don Sawyer, I believe."

He turned and climbed up a worn ladder out of the pit. As he emerged, I saw he was a slight, younger man. He walked over to the beer, picked up a bottle, fit a screwdriver under the cap and flipped it three feet in the air in a single, deft movement. He tossed his head back and the beer gurgled noisily down his throat.

"Ahh," he grinned. "Would you like a beer, Mr. Sawyer?"

I did, so he popped off another cap with the same quick jerk of the screwdriver. He pressed the warm bottle into my hand, cleared some debris from a corner of the workbench and leaned on his elbow. The bench, held up by a few feeble braces nailed to the bare studs, groaned a warning, but Morgan seemed oblivious to it. After finishing his beer, he wiped his greasy hands on his equally greasy coveralls and shook my hand.

"I'm Morgan Pearce. What can I do for you?"

Could I trust my SAAB to this man? How could anyone work in the midst of such a cluttered mess? I wondered how he could even find his tools. "Well, uh, I've got a problem with my car. The coil is split and the spark is grounding out."

"You have that little two-cycle job, don't you?" he asked, interest gleaming in his eyes. "Let's have a look at it."

We walked out and opened the hood. He looked excitedly at the engine, and didn't laugh once. He looked up at me, smiling. "That's the neatest little engine I've ever seen. How big is it?"

"I think it's something like 450 cc. It puts out thirty-six horse-power."

"Isn't that something," he said gleefully. My estimation of Morgan was improving rapidly. He looked at the coil, then returned to the garage, where he dug out several loose-leaf binders that had been buried beneath the mountains of clutter on the bench. He leafed familiarly through the grease-smeared pages.

"I'm afraid, Don, that they don't even list your car." I had a sudden vision of the car laid up for a month while I ordered a part from the States. "But," he went on, "I think I can make it work with a Volkswagen coil."

"You do?" I asked uncertainly.

"Well, we'll try anything," he said cheerily.

"Morgan can either find or make a part for any car on the road," a voice said from the other side of the car. "Why, I once broke the drive shaft on my pick-up; couldn't get another one anywhere. So Morgan here went down to the dump, found an old Dodge car, pulled the shaft, made it fit my truck and I'm still driving it, four years later."

"Well, O.K. then," I said, feeling more confidence in the man. "And by the way, I've been having a 'missing' problem with the car for a year now. Would you have a look at that too? Oh yeah, and my gas gauge is broken."

Morgan began to clamber back down the ladder to the cata-comb below. "O.K."

"When can I pick it up, Morgan?"

"I'm going into Gander tomorrow, so if I get back in time I should have it ready for you tomorrow after supper."

I walked back down the hill towards the Pikes' garden, feeling relieved. I had found myself a mechanic. As I strolled along, a boy on a bicycle rode up beside me. It was Benjamin Collins. "Howdy, Mr. Sawyer."

"Hi, Ben." After better than a month, I no longer needed Warrick as a full time interpreter to understand Ben, though I still had to ask him to repeat any sentence longer than a few words.

"O.K. Listen, Mr. Sawyer, would it be all right if I stopped by to see you and Mrs. Sawyer sometime?"

"Sure, Ben. Any time. Just come on over, we'll probably be there."

He smiled. "Thanks. See you later."

That night we had Doreen over for dinner. In fact, there had been rather few nights when Doreen had not been over for dinner, since we had managed to persuade May Pike that much as we appreciated her cooking we were able to get dinner for ourselves. Doreen, it seemed, was going crazy. Depressed and terribly lonely, she would sit on our couch and hang her head, her light brown hair hanging limply across her face, looking like a dejected Afghan dog. She found both the school and the loneliness equally crushing.

The only thing that seemed to pull her out of her depression was enormous quantities of Gamza wine, which we consumed with abandon. "Let's pretend we're in Paris," she would say, pirouetting around the room to the tinny sounds of our little cassette tape recorder while sipping wine from a plastic juice glass.

This night, however, Doreen was in a different mood. After several days of suppressed excitement, she finally spat it out—she was falling in love. Her first Newfoundland love had been a curly-haired boy in my grade eight class whom she insisted on referring to as "Young Bacchus." After we had talked her out of this fantasy, she turned her attention outside the school.

In this way she had found Ivan Ryder, the confused eighteen-year-old son of a local businessman and bulwark of the Salvation Army. Ivan had spent time in Toronto and St. John's in a band and was now playing behind strippers in a sleazy night club near Warrendale. But no amount of sober analysis was going to dampen Doreen's romance this time. She bubbled with excitement.

We were talking with Doreen when a knock came at the door. Benjamin Collins stood smiling in the hall. "Come on in, Ben," I said.

"I was just walking along the lane with Warrick and Kevin and thought I'd stop in and say hello."

"Great. Why didn't Warrick and Kevin come in too?"

Ben laughed. "Kevin might have but Warrick said no, absolutely not, sir. He vowed he'd never set foot in a teacher's house as long as he lives. He says they're all the same—demons."

Ben hardly said another word for the rest of the evening. He sat in the corner and read comics and *Playboy*. When I went out a short time later, however, Ben seemed to feel that I had left him in charge. While I was gone, the sink pipe separated as Jan was doing the dishes, allowing soapy water to flood across the floor. Already somewhat giddy from the wine, Jan and Doreen responded with hysterical laughter, but, according to Jan, Ben hardly batted an eye. He just started to calmly mop up the water. As soon as I returned, he left for home.

The next day after supper I had Roger give me a ride up to Morgan's. When I entered, I found Morgan still tinkering with my car, two new men sitting alongside drinking beer. I sat down on an empty car wheel.

"Well, Don, I put the new coil on and it works fine, and I got your gas gauge operating again. Just a loose wire." I got up to look under the hood to see that the coil had been remounted with a strap on the side of the engine compartment. "I also checked out your miss. Everything is fine as far as I can see, so it has to be this." He pointed to a hole in the distributor cap with a short length of hose extending from it. "This must be some sort of vent hole, but the way it is here, the hose just allows moisture and water to pour straight into the distributor. That's why it only acted up in the rain.

"Order another one—this one's cracked slightly anyway—and we'll see if it's got that fifth hole. In any case, for now we'll simply seal it off and that should take care of your problem."

And it did. I had had the car into SAAB mechanics from Seattle, Washington, to Flint, Michigan, and none had been able to fix it. Then this man, never having seen a SAAB before, had spotted the problem almost immediately.

I sat back on the car wheel while Morgan plunked the hood down. Before I had settled, a warm beer was placed in my hand by one of the other men. Morgan wiped his hands on his overalls and squatted down near the front of the car.

"That's pretty amazing, Morgan, that you found that when a dozen other mechanics haven't."

"Our Morgan is a very clever fellow," said an older man with a grey mustache.

"Not a'tall." Morgan scrunched up his face in protest.

"That's true, though, just the same, Morgan boy," The other man said. He looked at me. "You know those water barrels between bicycle wheels?" I nodded. He was referring to the water carts we had seen around town since the first day: they were barrels slung between two bicycle wheels with handles extending from the frame. The barrel remained level, pivoting on pins, regardless of the angle of the handles. "Well, those are in use all over Newfoundland. And you know who invented them?"

"Morgan?"

"He surely did, sir."

"Ah, George, go on with you. That was nothing."

"Nothing, he says. When I was a boy we used to haul barrels on wagons. When Morgan was thirteen he built the first bicycle tire barrel. The barrel never tips, you see. It was a real comfort. Hell, I used to have to dump out one barrel for every one I got home."

"Why'd you have to dump it out?" I asked.

"Well," the man said, a little sheepishly, "there's a custom here that if you spill any water on the ground the whole barrel is spoiled, so you have to dump the whole works out."

We all drank in silence for a moment. Then Bill, another of the men present, began. "There was this fella come through here about fifteen years ago, he was a professor from the University of Toronto. Anyway, he came out here to study how the natives live." This last was delivered in a pompous British accent. "He settled in Thornton one summer, but he came up here too, poking around, asking questions and writing it all down.

"Well, I knew the people he boarded with down in Thornton, and they fed him the biggest pack of lies you've ever heard. About people being eaten alive by two-hundred pound cod fish and times when the whole town lived a month on a single moose liver." Everyone was laughing now, since they had already heard the story. "And the bloody fool went and printed it all," Bill finished in feigned amazement.

"They used to sit around the table reading his book out loud and laughing till they cried."

Whatever the topic, among the men in his garage Morgan was the voice of reason. He would rarely contradict someone outright, though he would sometimes later confide quietly to me that "Buddy there tonight wouldn't know the truth if he met it in the road," but the men would often look to Morgan to put the issue into perspective, to provide the final analysis. Sometimes it would be a simple, "Yes, boy," but other times Morgan would lay out some of his own ideas.

To Jan's occasional irritation, from that night on I spent many evenings sipping beer in Morgan's garage, talking with him and anyone else who stopped in about engines, transmissions, provincial premier Joey Smallwood, what had been and what was coming. Sometimes I would have the SAAB develop a rattle or a clunk as an excuse for a visit, but more often I would just pull in to say hello, have a warm beer thrust into my hand and be drawn into the yarns and debates that seemed to fill the garage as constantly as the clutter and grease.

Unfortunately for Jan, there was no woman's equivalent to Morgan's garage. Except for Doreen, who had her own problems, Jan felt out of touch with most of the women in the community. "It's not that I don't like them," she said to me "I do. It's just that our experiences have been so different. There's not that much to say to each other."

One afternoon as I picked her up at school after work, she got into the car shaking her head. "I just don't know," she sighed.

"What's wrong?"

"Oh, nothing really. Marcia just asked me down to see her classroom. She'd decorated it for Thanksgiving."

"Yeah?"

"What she'd done was hang thirty pictures of turkeys all over the room. Mimeographed turkeys that the kids had coloured."

"What's wrong with that?"

"Nothing, except that they were all exactly the same. The birds were brown, the grass was green, the sun was yellow, the sky was blue. 'Isn't it nice that they're all the same?' she asked me.

Then she showed me a couple on her desk. One turkey was blue with a black head and the other one had bands of yellow, red, pink and orange. 'Look at these,' she told me in disgust. 'Turkeys aren't blue.'"

Personally, I was constantly amazed by the creativity and ingenuity of Jan's kids. One night she brought home a stack of pictures. "Look at these. Do you know what they are?"

They were obviously frogs. Their heavy round bodies were bounding all over the papers on long, springy legs. Each was different, but they were unmistakably frogs. As I looked at these delightful creatures, I thought about one of my early experiences in my Art 7 class. "O.K. kids," I had said as I passed out paper and pencils. "Today we're each going to use our imagination and design our dream house, complete with a floor plan." Everyone looked at me dubiously. I explained the idea of a floor plan, showed examples, and began to sketch one of my own ideas on the board—a circular house on a column that rotated. I was enthusiastically designing rooms, sticking in elevators and circular beds, and everyone was staring at me blankly.

"O.K., got the idea? Just let your imagination go and come up with a sketch of the greatest house you can think of, no matter how outrageous it is."

As I walked around trying to generate enthusiasm, the kids sat and looked uncertainly at each other. Finally I stopped by one girl's desk. She was drawing a one-dimensional square house with a peaked roof, a smoking chimney, one door and three windows with curtains.

"Is this really your dream house?" I asked.

"No," she replied hesitantly, "but it's the only house I know how to draw." Two thirds of the students apparently felt the same way, as they turned out identical drawings.

"You know, Norman," I said later in the staff room. "It's too damned bad that these kids have had their creativity so totally demolished. I'd sure like to see some more money for art equipment so I can get them working in other media, like clay, paint and leather. Maybe that way we can begin to help them regain their..."

"Don," Norman broke in. "We just don't have the money for that kind of thing. Anyway," he went on, "we had a professional artist here a few years ago and he said not more than five per cent of these kids have any real talent. So can we justify spending money on the rest? No one's going to get a job in art."

I was aghast. "Jobs can hardly be the sole criterion for determining what we do in school," I said. "What good are mathematical principles"—Norman was a math teacher—"if the kids don't come out with enough confidence and imagination to use their skills effectively?"

What ensued was the opening round of a debate on the purposes of education that raged for almost two years. This time Norman lined up Calvin to bolster his position ("I've worked with those kids in Art, tried to teach them perspective, and they just don't have any talent"), and the rest of the staff watched with interest.

Our argument reached a temporary climax with our first staff meeting a few days later. This was the meeting where the marks each teacher had given to his classes were considered and discussed by all the staff. "Don," I had been told repeatedly, "grade them hard the first term." "Flunk the whole bloody bunch," Willis laughed. "It'll make them work harder for the rest of the year. You can always ease off later." But I could not see it. I wanted my students to articulate their ideas without fear of reprisal. I did not intend to reward them for thinking like me, just for thinking.

I was beginning to believe, though I did not fully understand it at the time, what a teacher told me later: "A classroom is a microcosmic society; what you are is what you teach, and what you say is a lot less important than what you do. If you believe in the principles of democracy and humanism you'd better operate a democratic, humane classroom or you're contradicting those values. Likewise, if you believe in the integrity of the individual and the acceptance of differences, but use punishment and reward to coerce students into compliance with your views and needs, you are teaching the need for submission and conformity."

Furthermore, as we moved into November, the kids really were beginning to open up and express themselves. We spent whole periods in rambling, animated discussion. The students and I decided we had become tired of sitting in straight rows, directing attention to the front and forcing students to shout over the heads of others or to swivel in their seats, so we began to try out various seating arrangements. With my eights we also established a policy where, at any time, any student could demand a circle discussion. If the other students agreed that the subject needed immediate attention, we broke off whatever we were doing and took up the problem. It only happened a few times, but the experience helped people to be less shy about speaking out and shifted a measure of classroom control to the students themselves.

I had also begun what we called an impressions book, a notebook kept by each student in which he wrote responses to specific experiences, such as short "sensory awareness" field trips, films, and tapes of unusual music. I tried to offer at least one such writing experience each week. Early in the fall, after spending time talking with the eights about apprehending the world through our senses and expressing our perceptions in concrete language, I passed out sheets lined with five columns, one for each sense. "O.K.," I told the class, "it's bright and warm out today, so what we're going to do is go outside this period, find a quiet spot somewhere around the school, and concentrate on our surroundings through each sense. Write down your perceptions in the appropriate columns, then, when we come back, take those data and write a short descriptive essay on the experience. O.K.?" That seemed straightforward enough. "Let's go."

Everybody sat uneasily, eyeing me in bewilderment. "Well, let's go," I repeated.

"Outside?"

"Yeah, outside. What's wrong?"

"We've never gone outside before during school. Are you sure we can do it?"

I was, once again, astounded. "Your mean you've never been on a field trip?"

"Once, in fourth grade," someone offered, "we went to the public library."

We left the room, each class staring at us in amazement as we passed. But once outside, the kids, even those who had been afraid to write much more than their name, wrote like mad. They crawled over the roots and stones and spread out in the marsh, peering intently at the lichen "growing like a tiny garden" on the rocks; they listened for the dull booming of the waves that washed in from the sea.

When I collected the books for the first marking period I discovered some remarkable writing. Some of it was deeply personal and much of it highly imaginative. From it I received a glimpse of the writers' personalities and feelings as well as their writing. One theme appeared with surprising frequency: enmity for the school. One of the kids had written an essay on our short trip outside that went in part:

> I just escaped from a terrible place, a planet of knowledge, but I found no knowledge so I had to escape. Into a world of Green, Green and Green. I took off my sandals and walked threw a big green carpet which seemed to go on forever. My world was rusty and red but this beautiful world was so green and bright that my eyes started to hurt because my world was so dark and gloomy.
> The air was fresh and clean. I lay down on the lovely green carpet and started to live. All I had to do was lie down and dream and things came into my mind that never would have come their if I was back in my old world. My dreams were so beautiful and bright, not like the dreams I had in my other world. I listened and I heard a lot of nice sounds. Some little animals were busy hopping about and making happy little noises. The wind was blowing but so gently that it felt so good and made a lovely sound as it swished gently through the trees.

Reading the students' essays, I suddenly perceived that I had missed an obvious point of departure. In many classes, instead of focussing on the school and the process of education—the most salient aspect of our common environment—I had been trying to open up a dialogue on concepts which were abstract and alien. Why not make the school itself a part of the curriculm? I decided to try it.

As another stimulus for writing, I had brought in a number of tapes, one of which was a semi-hypnotic song called "Space Walk" that, through the use of synthesizers and lyrics, placed the listener on the moon as the earth and stars spun in space. I had asked the students to jot down the images they saw and felt as they listened to the song. When I flipped through Kevin Fillier's impressions book, I was arrested by the page of images and graphics he had composed in response to the song. With a split sphere he had illustrated how sounds and imagination create "enter locking empulses." A line of arcs traced the path of "a ball of sound bouncing." Convincing proof of an original mind, but how was I supposed to grade it?

I felt equally good about what was taking place in grade ten. In history we were slowly moving to a course that examined the immediate social environment in Hoberly Cove and the role of the school and community. Here again, we were talking about what school, history and English should be, instead of what it was.

I wrote my first Deep Thought Quiz for the grade tens, asking them what they thought of the proposition that learning should prepare students to deal with the world they live in. The quiz probed for detail: What questions was life posing for them? How might school help answer these questions, and what skills and knowledge would be of value then and later? How much had they been helped by school in the past? The quiz also asked what, in their opinion, constituted a significant learning experience; what they were lately thinking about; how their attitudes had changed since the beginning of grade nine. This type of inquiry elicited lengthy, interesting replies. In response to one question, a girl wrote:

> I cannot see the point of a student studying a subject in school just so that he'll pass a grade. I think a person should learn in school how to get along in the world around him be-

cause this is the one thing he is going to have to be able to do.

As far as I am now, my past education has not helped me to deal with my problems. Although I've passed all my grades it hasn't helped me one little bit with the problems I have. My problems outside don't have anything to do with what I have learned. I have never learned to think, until this year, but just memorize, and when I started to face my problems I just had to think. I tell you, it was mighty hard and a bit frightening.

Everything that I do learn I forget after going to another grade, so did that help me? It didn't help me at all. What I have learned, from my family and friends, has helped me to better cope with my problems than anything I have learned since I started school. They are the kind of people I will have to live with in the future and the kind of people I will have to learn from. I think they are and will be more imortant to my learning than what school has ever been or ever will be.

I feel that to deal with my present and future I need to develop an education that will help me take responsibility, teach me how to cope with my problems and how to get along with others in this world. These are the things that I will need to know when I get out of school. Not only when I graduate, but I need to know them right now.

I began giving one to three plusses for thought and effort as a sort of compromise mark. No matter how I looked at it, I could not justify failing any of my kids in English. In history? Maybe one student, who had done nothing; but that was mainly a problem of adjustment, as much my fault as his. So I submitted my grades, passing everyone, and waited to see what Norman's response would be.

No one spoke to me the entire day of the staff meeting. To heighten the tension, Russell Taylor was supposed to come out for the meeting.

The last period before the end of school that day I taught Geography. Because the students had never tried group work, I had split them up into co-operative units as much as possible. This day, they were working in three large groups, each one responsible for a section of Africa. We had gridded out each portion of an African map from the geography book (one inch to one foot) onto three enormous sheets of wrapping paper, and each student had mapped his country with rivers, cities, etc. Now, on completing the preliminaries, we had three sections of Africa which *should* fit together when cut out, and they were lying on the gym floor like pieces of an enormous jigsaw puzzle. How we were going to mesh them was beyond me. Thirty-five kids each had his or her own idea, and they were arguing around the fringes when another student notified me that I was wanted in the office.

I gave everyone a confident grin. "I know you can figure it out," I said. "I'll be back in a while."

Norman was waiting for me, holding my grade sheet in his hand. "You know, Don," he said in a severe tone, "I don't see how you can pass all these kids in English. It makes grades worthless. Why, some of these students can hardly read."

"That's true, Norman, and as long as they're told they can't read and are made to feel incapable of learning, they probably won't improve much, either."

Norman's face was grim. "The rest of us are trying to maintain some sort of standards, Don. This sort of thing makes us look foolish."

"I guess you and I are just giving grades for different reasons, Norman," I said. "Since the same kids seem to be given the good grades or the bad grades year after year, it all seems a little foolish anyway. I mean, all that does is sort kids on the basis of their reading or knowledge level, which we already know. That doesn't seem like teaching to me, just testing. You see what I mean?"

Norman obviously did not. "Why are you giving grades at all, then?" he demanded in a high, tight voice. I had noticed that when Norman got upset his face would redden noticeably and his eyes would cloud.

"Well," I started, thinking about the question, "I guess because I have to." Norman's eyes bulged a little and his flushed face turned suddenly pale. An uneasy silence fell over the cluttered room. Before he could respond, the bell rang in the halls. A cluster of kids formed around the door, knocking urgently. Norman stalked to the door. "Yes?" he asked crisply.

"We want to see Mr. Sawyer."

Norman gestured with his head at the door, where six or seven of the eighth graders were standing outside. "Mr. Sawyer," Roland Fillier began, "once we managed to shut Warrick up we got things going pretty well. So we want to stay after school and work on it, O.K.?"

"Sure. How many?"

"Oh, fifteen or so."

"Do you need any help?" I asked hopefully.

"Naw. We'll let you know when we're done." They walked back down the hall, arguing among themselves. "Listen, Warrick boy," I heard Roland yell. "You're not the only one who's got ideas, sure!"

Other teachers filtered into the staff room, postponing a renewal of the argument with Norman. A few minutes later, Russell Taylor walked in. He greeted me warmly, then turned to the rest of the assembled staff. Alpheaus gave him a bright smile and Roger shook his hand, but everyone else treated him with polite indifference.

Russell began by reviewing the freedom we now had, unshackled by public exams, to interpret the curriculum as we saw fit. "I hope we can make the subjects better serve the students," he concluded. I concurred enthusiastically and began to rattle off some of the plans I had for extending the classroom to incorporate the entire community. I realized how desperate I was to have someone faintly positive to talk to. As I rambled on, it occurred to me that Russell and I were carrying on a dialogue; everyone else sat and regarded me with either mild curiosity or chilly hostility. I faltered in mid-sentence and trailed off lamely. The same coolness I had seen towards Russell was now being directed towards me.

"Let's get down to the grades," Norman said brusquely. This was the sign for Russell's departure. He and his outside ideas had been dismissed. He sighed and rose to leave as a delegation of chattering eights formed again around the door. I got up to talk to them, thankful for the opportunity to ease the tension.

"Mr. Sawyer," Roland whispered hoarsely, as if a staff meeting was too sacrosanct to be disturbed by students speaking in normal tones. "We've finished the map. Come have a look."

As Russell was leaving anyway, I invited him down to the room. The map was gorgeous. Fifteen faces, lit with pride, spread before it in a semicircle. It hung, all 120 square feet of it, like a ragged, variegated quilt. And the three pieces I had left lying hopelessly separated on the floor had been grafted together so that hardly a seam could be detected.

When Russell walked in, the excited group fell quiet and watched him uncertainly. He looked at the map, which covered half the wall, beamed, then addressed the group. "Very nice. I guess geography is a lot more fun this year, eh?"

Everyone looked at him mutely. I wanted to kick Roland, who would usually never shut up. "Sure, Mr. Taylor," I wanted him to say. "Geography is great this year. Mr. Sawyer is the greatest teacher since Jesus. We love every minute." But the silence around us only deepened.

"I guess you've been following the news about Africa in class, eh?" Not a sound from the students, even though we had spent the whole week talking about what was going on. I smiled at Roland, then bared my teeth once I had caught his eye. Roland nodded his head vaguely. "Then did you hear what happened in Angola today?" Russell asked, looking at Roland. Hell, Angola was Roland's country. He had spent half of yesterday's class explaining to us the status of the various liberation groups, complete with leaders' names and relative strengths, in their struggle against the Portuguese. Now he stood there dumbly, staring at his feet. Finally he mumbled something under his breath, which Russell accepted as an answer. He congratulated them on the map, said goodbye to me and left.

As soon as he cleared the door the group became its usual garrulous self. "Roland, why didn't you say something?" I asked exasperatedly.

"Aw, those big shots make me nervous. What do you think of the map?" he asked brightly.

It really was beautiful. I seriously doubted that I could have put the thing together as capably as they had. "How'd you figure out how to piece it together so well?" I asked in admiration.

"Oh, we just all got together and fit it like a shoe. Warrick finally got so mad he left, but that was O.K. because no one was listening to his bawling anyway. We had to bend a few boundaries," he pointed out—I had noticed Tanzania's shrunken condition—"but it looks pretty good, don't you think?"

Buoyed by the success of that venture, I re-entered the staff meeting in a better state of mind. My outlook did not last long. As other teachers read off their grades, it became clear that almost no students would escape unscathed. Virtually every kid was receiving one or more failures, some as many as five. Kids whom I had seen beginning to break out of their shells, who were fingering the new books we had just received in the library or beginning to write for the first time, were being slapped with their customary failures.

Finally, I questioned the purpose of such grading. Calvin glowered at me. "You can throw standards out the window, let your students run wild and not make them learn anything if you like," he said indignantly. "But I'll be damned if any kid will pass my class unless he works for it."

"I'm not suggesting that students shouldn't work to pass a class, Calvin. I'm just saying that what is acceptable work must vary from student to student. Otherwise we're condemning half of the kids to perpetual failure. It seems to me we should be interested in raising the collective ability level of our classes, rather than pitting one student against another."

"And what'll we end up with then? People who graduate who can't read or do simple math?" Norman demanded.

"We're flunking out kids who can't do those things now. The point is, I don't think it's our responsibility to certify and classify students. That's testing, pure and simple. If employers want to determine a person's competence for a job, fine, let them establish their own criteria and measurements. We're not here to serve them, we're here to serve the students and the community."

To my surprise, though I was the only active dissenter, Willis and Alpheaus seemed to be listening intently. Doreen and Roger were nodding tacit support.

"That's crap," Calvin said. His hulking shoulders leaned forward and his face darkened. "I give every kid an equal chance in my class, and if they don't make it that's their fault, not mine. And I'll be damned if I'll let some loafer get by so I won't hurt his feelings."

"You have to remember, Don," Norman said conciliatingly, "that some of these kids just don't have what it takes. They just aren't bright enough to master the work."

"Well, Norman, I don't really believe that. I think that everyone has pretty much the same potential intelligence, with occasional and obvious exceptions, and that experience and environment are what make the major difference in performance." Calvin snorted in disgust and Norman smiled condescendingly. "Now that's my belief," I went on. "But whether I'm right or not isn't that important. It seems to me that in any case our job and our responsibility is to provide each kid, regardless of his academic background or level of achievement, with as positive an educational and personal experience as possible. Anything we do which makes him feel bad about himself or which reduces his desire to learn is harmful and should be avoided. And these grades are cutting these kids up in ribbons."

Norman growled, "It's getting too late to hash all this out now. Let's get these grades out of the way and get out of here."

We continued, and my grades were accepted without further comment. Hardly a dozen more words were exchanged. The meeting broke up and I left confused and dismayed. Maybe the others were right. Who was I to come into their town fresh out of a university four thousand miles away and tell them how to operate the school? Maybe my brashness and attitude did stem from my lack of experience.

After dinner I walked up the hill to Morgan's in the cold November night. I went in and sat down and took a proffered beer. After a while Morgan poked his head out from below the car he was working on. "What's wrong, my son?" he said in mock concern. "Did your little wife turn you down tonight?" He laughed, his cigarette shaking its ashes off into the pit. He then repeated one of his favourite bits of philosophy. "If you don't have it bad once in a while, how do you know when you have it good?"

"Don, boy," he went on seriously. "I don't know what you're doing in school there, but Curtis seems to like it." Curtis, Morgan's oldest son, was in my eighth grade classes.

"He brought an old comic book home one night and said you'd given it to him in English class. Well, I nearly died. But then I saw him working on his story the other evening, and I couldn't believe it. I've never seen Curtis write a thing since he started going to school." Morgan laughed again, then stuck his head out and looked at me. "I read it, and it was some good, too."

"Yes, boy," someone else said from the dark. "You're doing fine."

6

"We Love Thee, Newfoundland"

By late October, winter had begun to close on the town, and the rest of the world became a vague rumour. Even the FLQ crisis, though beamed into every home, felt remote, like a drama in northern Ireland.

We visited St. John's with Doreen, but it did little to dispel our feelings of being cut off from the energy flow, the movement, of the continent. In fact, it seemed to heighten our sense of isolation. St. John's had the feel of a capital, but the capital of a small ancient kingdom tucked high and deep in the Himalayas. It bore little resemblance to the rest of Canada I had seen, appearing more like the huge Newfoundland outport it is. If we were unable to find something in St. John's, it was simply unavailable anywhere on the island. And a great many things fit into that category. The yellow legal-length writing pads that I liked to use were not to be had in any of the three office supply stores. My favourite pipe tobacco was not imported into the province. And no amount of searching could unearth a decent bookstore.

We had been growing steadily more aware of the degree of Newfoundland nationalism alive in the province. Though few people still argued the wisdom of aligning with Canada, the old Newfoundland flag flew with far more frequency than the maple leaf. One family in Hoberly Cove, for reasons that I could never ascertain, insisted on flying the French tricolour. Non-Newfoundlanders were referred to as Americans, Canadians or, more commonly, mainlanders. It was not unusual to hear someone say, "That feller there came over for a visit from Canada."

An example of the Newfoundlanders' lingering feelings of nationalism, or at least their enduring pride, occurred at a speech contest in Thornton. Somehow I, along with Norman, had been persuaded to act as a judge, and so the two of us wedged ourselves amidst half of Thornton into the Thornton high school gym, which was even smaller than Hoberly Cove's. Prior to the contest a woman strode to the piano to play the national anthem. I stood up, and was going over the first stanza of "O Canada" in my head when a few bars of a totally foreign song tinkled from the piano. Without the least hesitation the crowd launched into "Ode to Newfoundland." They sang three verses, each more lustily than the former, and when they sang, two hundred voices strong, "We love thee, we love thee, we love thee, Newfoundland," emotion surged through the auditorium.

In early October two friends of ours, Pete and Janey Pitchford, came up to visit us from Michigan at the beginning of an eight-month honeymoon tour. They had sent us a letter that they were on the way, but we had no chance to give them exact directions, so when they knocked at the door I was curious about how they had managed to find us.

"Oh," laughed Peter, "we just stopped some guy along the road and asked him if he knew where the Sawyers lived. He scratched his head and said, 'You mean those new teachers with the funny little blue car? They stay with Carl Pike.' And here we are."

With them we bumped into Sam Pritchett again. He invited us all over to his little shack by the community wharf, which he said we would recognize by the moose antlers nailed on the front,

85

to sample some of his home brew. Jan, displaying continued good judgement, said she didn't care to attend. But the Pitchfords were enthusiastic, and I had never had home brew before, so we decided to stop over for just an hour or so.

We were greeted at the door by Sam, who led us through a low shed crowded with lobster traps and fishing gear to a tiny and even lower room in the back. This was Sam's home. He heated the place with a small cast-iron wood stove which took up about a quarter of the floor space. The remainder of the room was devoted to an old metal bed piled with pulp magazines, a short counter with a wash basin, two patched, wooden chairs, and two ten-gallon plastic pails of beer.

Sam gave us each a cup, then opened up one of the white plastic pails, revealing a thin yellowish liquid with a white scum on top. He dipped a plastic pitcher into the fluid and poured each of our cups full.

It was horrible. The stuff tasted like rancid cider. "What's in this, Sam?" I asked, wondering what combination of ingredients could possibly produce such a vile excuse for beer.

"Well, I tried just about everything," he slurred, "but in the end I decided that the simplest recipe is the best. All I use is ten gallons of water, five pounds of sugar and two packages of yeast, let it work for a few days, and it's ready to drink."

"You mean you don't add malt, hops, rice or barley or anything?" My knowledge of the brewer's art was limited, but I knew something was definitely missing. I hadn't expected Sam's specialty to be aged in beechwood kegs, but this was ridiculous.

"Not a thing," he grinned. "And it still has the kick of a nasty horse."

As I choked down three or four cups, I had to agree. Eventually it seemed like a good idea to take a tub of beer over to Sam's brother's house and to finish the evening there. "The only beer I've got left is a little green," he mused uncertainly. "But it should be O.K."

Sam led us up a worn trail to a yellow and green house set back among the rocks. The simple warmth of other Newfoundland homes was absent here, and even in my semiconscious state the starkness of the interior assaulted me. There were no shades or curtains on the windows, and patterned linoleum covered the floors. There were three small bedrooms off the kitchen-living room, two of them apparently sleeping quarters for the seven children, but none had doors. Bare two-by-four studs framed the simple beds and sparse furnishings inside. A blanket hung across the doorway into the adults' bedroom.

All but the oldest of the children were already crowded into the beds, two or three to a single mattress, tossing restlessly. Occasionally one would get up and walk groggily to a rough closet where slop jars served as toilets and another grey blanket provided a measure of privacy.

Sam's brother, Cyril, was a gruff man who at first seemed awed by having a teacher in the house. He had his wife hopping around digging out biscuits and margarine, despite our protests. She sat all evening, uneasy and timid on the fringes of the conversation, never raising her voice or laughing too hard.

As the level of the beer, visible on the side of the bucket, sank towards the floor, Cyril became increasingly loud. He began talking about cutting wood for the stove in the "hats" behind the town. "I used a buck saw for years," he bellowed, "but now I have a chain saw I fixed. You wanna see it?" Cyril stumbled out the door onto the back porch and lugged in a battered antique chain saw of considerable bulk. He dropped the heavy saw towards the floor and simultaneously yanked up on the wood handle attached to the starting cord. The saw erupted with a roar that pressed me back in my chair. Like a madman he began waving the thundering machine around the room, gunning the engine into screaming crescendoes.

Finally satisfied, Cyril shut the engine off and set the saw in the middle of the table. Acrid blue smoke filled the room, adding to my growing nausea. I had had enough. I mumbled some sort of thanks to the Pritchetts and collected Peter and Janey, who were almost as drunk and otherwise stunned as I was.

Jan awoke me out of my stupor at 7:00 the next morning. We were participating in a volleyball tournament that Saturday in Northport, a town about twenty miles away, and as coach I had to be there. Panic filled me: I had heard of going blind on home brew, and now it had happened. I tried to stand up, but my knee crumpled beneath me in pain and my head felt like the proverbial pink cotton candy being spun on a stick. I groaned, crawled sightless to the bathroom, and collapsed in semiconsciousness on the bathroom floor.

I slowly came to, still unable to see. Finally one eyelid, which had been stuck shut, unglued itself and wavered open. Though the room was furry and indistinct, at least I was not totally blind. Still, it was only with Jan's assistance that I eventually managed to stand and wash myself. Even after an hour I was too sick to remain upright longer than a few minutes, and the world still looked heavily veiled. But I had to make it to the tournament.

Volleyball had become an important part of my teaching life. I had approached the sport with considerable reservation, and my coaching reflected it. My input was limited to casual observation and occasional play. I slowly learned the game, but was totally unprepared for the ordeal of the first competition.

We had opened the season in Warrendale, a school twice the size of Hoberly Cove whose team was coached by Harry Stringer, Squire Memorial's former coach. To prove his coaching talent, Harry desperately wanted to demolish his former team, and, unknown to me, the game had thus been turned into something of a grudge match. As soon as we walked into the packed gym, however, I realized that this brand of volleyball was very different from the easy, meandering game I remembered. Hundreds of Warrendale students, spurred on by a squad of squealing, cavorting cheerleaders, were screaming for blood. Their team was already in the midst of a snappy spiking drill, smacking sets to the court below. Its coach stood watching us with a sneer.

Our players were obviously out-psyched. We had prepared no pre-game routine; in fact, I thought ruefully, we had prepared little for the game in general. We had done almost no conditioning and, because of my ignorance, had not drilled extensively in any of the basics. The match was four out of seven—a long, tiring night. I quickly huddled with the captains and put together a line-up, which we ran to the timekeeper, and the games started.

I had never seen volleyball played like this. Our players were sliding across the floor and climbing into the stands to make saves. Sweat poured down their faces as they strained to smash the ball over the net. Jeff Fillier lunged all over the floor time after time, throwing himself across the court to bring certain points back into play. Reg Pritchett stretched his full six feet two inches and, helped by perfect soft sets, crashed thunderous spikes through the opposing players. My heart pounded and huge perspiration circles began to spread under my arms.

Still, we lost the first game. Calls against us that were close seemed to occur with increasing frequency, while calls against Warrendale were met with a barrage of boos and such angry displays by their coach, who stomped continually up to the referee, screaming in his face, that they seemed to almost disappear. Finally in the second game I broke. A Warrendale player had hit the ball with his knee and our players, thinking the ball dead, had not returned it. The referee called it a point for Warrendale. Jeff protested from the floor.

I didn't know the rule, but if Jeff said that a call was illegal, I was going to back him up. I stomped across the court and confronted the referee, complaining vehemently. In the middle of the discussion, Stringer pushed his way through and started screaming at me and the referee.

My temper gave way and I lost all caution about bluffing. "It's illegal to hit the ball with any part of the body below the waist," I shouted back. "You should know that, if you're such a hot-shot volleyball player."

We had argued for five minutes when a student trotted up with a rule book. Much to my amazement, I was right. We were awarded the serve and as I walked back across the court our rooters cheered until the floor shook. The players surrounded me, smiling broadly and slapping me on the back. I had just become their coach.

The Northport tournament was our first big-league tournament and our first opportunity to play arch-rival Twillingate. Both Northport and Twillingate high schools were two or three times the size of Squire Memorial, but Hoberly Cove had a tradition of fielding gutsy teams. Somehow I had to get there. Kids had been calling the house since 8:00 (when it became clear that I was not going to make the bus) desperately concerned that I would not make it at all.

Peter drove us to the Northport school, where our players were already warming up. When I stumbled into the gym, my vision still blurry, the players clustered around me. At first they looked at my pale, drawn features with concern, but when a whistle shrilled and I pressed my hand to my forehead to stifle the pain, the team pretty accurately assessed the situation. For the rest of the day the boys showed amazing consideration, even avoiding raising their voices. And, considering that they were playing short an effective coach, they did well, beating Northport in three straight games and just losing to Twillingate two games to three.

A week later, when Jan and I drove up to Twillingate for another tournament, we took a couple of players with us. Brian Fillier, one of several sixteen-year-olds in grade eight, sat in the front seat as we headed towards Port Warford and the "Road to the Isles," a road which ended in the brief ferry trip to New World Island, where Twillingate was located. As we drove along, I questioned Brian about houses, names of ponds and places. Each inquiry met with the same answer: "I don't know." We crossed a causeway labelled "Dildo Run." Fascinated, I questioned Brian once more. "Do you know why this is named Dildo Run, Brian?"

Brian turned to me in exasperation. "Mr. Sawyer, I've never been more than five miles from Hoberly Cove in my life. I don't know as much about this area as you do." He turned back to the window, something akin to fright in his eyes. Incredibly, Brian quit school in the spring to look for work in Toronto.

But by Christmas, despite earlier predictions, only one of my students, Sherry Pritchett, had dropped out of grade eight. Sherry had flunked several grades and, I was told, was "definitely not academic material." She had begun to respond somewhat (she had blushed and hidden her head, grinning from ear to ear in pleasure, when I read one of her papers out in class), but

90

apparently I was not able to do enough to keep her in school. I asked Norman what she would end up doing if she left.

"Oh, she'll go to Gander and work as a maid. It's probably just as well; she wasn't getting anything out of school anyway. She'll learn the trade and do all right."

In three months she returned to Hoberly Cove, pregnant and alone.

Teachers, too, were beginning to resign. Judy gleefully informed us one evening that she was pregnant and would be quitting right after Christmas. Even more disturbing, Doreen, who had teetered on the edge of a complete breakdown for the last several months, had also had enough. Besides the loneliness and overall frustration, she was fed up with the condescension she was subjected to by some of the staff. Her opinions and ideas would be politely tolerated, then promptly ignored.

"I just can't stand being treated like a child any more," she confided. "They don't want any women in that school and they're doing their best to force me out. I know my quitting will only reinforce their attitudes towards women. Can't you hear it? 'Poor Doreen just couldn't stand up to the pressure. I guess women just don't have the stamina to take it.' But it's either quit or go crazy. I love the kids, but I hate the school."

This came as a real blow to Jan, who was already suffering from social withdrawal. Though the women continued to be extremely polite, Jan found it difficult to penetrate the rigid social tradition that defined a woman strictly in terms of her husband and children. The community had established very separate areas of responsibility and social activity for the sexes. Women's events were teas and baby and bridal showers. Men, in fact even male children, were rigorously excluded from these activities, as were women in parallel men's activities. Rarely would a man and woman be seen walking together, and outside of a dance, holding hands or other public displays of affection were almost unheard of.

Because there were so few alternatives available to the women of Hoberly Cove, most accepted their roles unquestioningly. But Jan could not, and often felt alien at women's functions. Most of the women Jan's age, twenty-two, already had two or three kids, and the conversation invariably revolved around their children. Furthermore, Jan felt that they were often uncomfortable with her.

"Women my age and even older insist on calling me Mrs. Sawyer," she said. "It's pretty hard to get close to people when they maintain such a distance."

She tried to break down some of the barriers by joining the only ongoing women's activity in town—the weight control club. But she weighed 105 pounds when she began, and she finally quit. "I just made them feel bad," she explained. "They've had a bunch of kids and are overweight, so they puff and groan doing sit-ups while I zip through my exercises."

Doreen had remained her closest friend in the community. And now she was leaving soon after Christmas.

The physical stiffness Jan noted in the older women was equally present in the kids, especially the girls. In physical education I was astonished to find that nearly half of my girls could not do a somersault. Because girls usually grew up with strict sanctions governing their physical activity, they were often awkward and very much out of touch with their bodies. I began doing free movement exercises ("Pretend you're a flower about to bloom. Listen to the music and grow upward towards the sun!") and dance. I had a hard time adjusting myself to the idea of prancing and pirouetting across the floor to my home-recorded sound track music from "2001" before fifteen or twenty tittering girls, but it was good for them to see a man trying to interpret music, I figured, and anyway it was kind of fun. Slowly we all began to lose our self-consciousness, and even the shyest, most overweight girl was dancing and swirling to "Also Sprach Zarathustra."

Jack Gibbons, the physical education co-ordinator from Gander, took pity on me and brought out some mats. On these we began to explore slightly more involved body movements such as the forward roll. Girls would run up to the mat and skid flat across the surface. Others would get their heads down all right but then freeze, their rears planted firmly in the air. But most of the kids loosened up quickly, and we were soon trying head stands and flips from rolled-up mats.

Jan, meanwhile, was doing exercises with her first grade kids every morning. Sometimes they would pretend they were clothes hanging on a line; other times they walked like ducks. She saw the kids develop a physical confidence and grace that was largely absent among the high school students. At the same time, her kids were participating in the overall operation of the classroom. Together they would decide when they would work on reading and when they would just play. "I always go in with an idea of what I'd like to accomplish," Jan explained, "but if it doesn't happen, then it doesn't happen."

Once I had stopped to pick Jan up shortly after 3:00. As I walked through the door to her class I was assaulted furiously by half a dozen kids waiting for the bus. "Don't step on the road!" they yelled. Holding my foot in midair I looked at a fantastic network of popsickle sticks that wound its way all over the classroom, over hills of carpeting, through forests of cut-out trees and around block villages. At railroad crossings tiny cut-out stop signs on sticks were stuck in Plasticine. A dozen kids were pushing dinky-toy cars and trucks through the complex, while others were pushing new roads into the dark frontiers of the room.

I stepped gingerly over the highway to where Jan was marking papers the kids had handed in. One showed Mr. Muggs, a dog from the first grade primer, calmly defecating on the ground. Another one had a wonderful picture of a giraffe munching on a tree. "A giraffe," it read, "lives in a zoo. And he likes the tree in the zoo. He eats the apples that bes on the trees. And he goes to sleep in the zoo. On a bed now. And he saws to me good night."

"How long has this been going on?" I motioned towards the highway department bulldozing a new section of road through the bookcase.

"About a week."

"How long are you going to leave it up?"

"Oh, they'll get tired of it after a while," she answered. "Then they'll take it apart and rearrange everything. A couple of weeks ago they built a mountain out of the wastebasket and ran the road up there. It was a real engineering marvel."

Jan had also built a small library, the only one in the school, of children's books. I noticed that several of the kids were giggling over *The Cat in the Hat*, ignoring the activity swarming on the floor around them.

One of the first things I had done in the high school was to form a library staff. I figured that a little early enthusiasm would go a long way towards cementing or, if necessary, obtaining funds to build some sort of library. But I was amazed at the extent of the interest. A simple note on the bulletin board brought thirty-five students to the first meeting. From there, we began planning operations. We arranged a timetable so that students would be completely in charge, devised a simple sign-out procedure in a scribbler, and laid plans to order books. I dug out old catalogues and new ones that had been ignored and had each member of the library staff circulate them, noting books requested. We had decided to buy only paperbacks because of the tremendous cost advantage.

When the money came through, we were set. Our first order was out before the end of September and our first three hundred books arrived soon after. With discounts and rebates, we were managing to average just a little over fifty cents a book. Though over half the books were fiction, we catalogued them roughly into six main areas, which seemed more than adequate for our needs. Soon after we had begun, a meteorologist from Gander visited the school for an address on vocations in meteorology. He was as appalled by the state of the library as I was, and pledged his entire two-hundred-volume collection of science fiction. We had added more than five hundred books in a little more than a month.

I began a branch of the Scholastic Book Club in school and every member agreed to put all free bonus books into the library. I also managed to cajole Norman into allocating enough money each month—twenty dollars—to purchase just about every book offered on the book club's high school list. Then we began a fund-raising drive that operated on and off for two years. The first approach was as successful as it was simple—we went door to door asking for donations. Later we became more sophisticated and ordered two hundred dollars' worth of chocolate bars. By Christmas we had brought in nearly a thousand books. Even more gratifying, in December an average of twenty books a day were being checked out, and more than a hundred kids had checked out at least one book. Though each student signed his book out and crossed his own name off when he returned it, we had lost virtually no books. The library staff students provided what supervision was necessary and took great pride in our slowly expanding collection. Every time another shipment came in, the day was like Christmas. A crowd would form at the door as the staff excitedly put out a display of the new books. They also made posters to cover the walls and replaced the desks with tables and chairs. For all its physical drabness, the library began to give off warmth and became a centre of the school.

Also I began structuring free reading time into my English classes. I kept a good collection of comics in the room, but the comic became increasingly less popular as the classes dove into their flashy new library paperbacks. I also began to ask for simple book reports, with some extraordinary results.

After a few months of nothing, I received a book report from Sterling Fillier (whose longest essay to that point had been a four-line disaster) that was three and a half pages long. It was largely a rambling, disjointed account of the book, and unfortunately the entire thing was written in three sentences, but he was writing! Sterling had discovered books, and after that I seldom saw him without two or three paperbacks. From that point on, his writing made slow but steady progress, and I looked back on those three and a half terrible pages of marathon run-on sentences as a milestone in my teaching.

In grade ten the distinctions between history and English were blurring, as had geography and English in grade eight. We had continued focussing on the school via several films, including *Summerhill,* which we treated as stimulus for class discussion and writing. Since many of the kids had a tough time conceiving of any genuine alternatives to the schooling they had always been exposed to, *Summerhill* provided an effective illustration of the ultimate critique. Some of the kids were repelled ("they all had dirty hands and faces"), some were enthralled, and some were indifferent. In any case, it provided a basis for discussion.

I had come to rely quite heavily on films, particularly the free offerings of the National Film Board (even though we had to pay return postage, an expense that did not make Norman too happy). Essentially the students were coming from a verbal, non-print-oriented background, and they seemed to relate very positively to film. They were remarkably observant and quickly saw subtle relationships and details in the films that I often missed.

Nonetheless, I was acutely aware that I, especially with the tens, was still maintaining a teacher-oriented classroom. We had changed the content, but I was still absolutely determining the direction. Students were not used to being asked to take responsibility for their own learning and were generally content to allow me to name the game so that they could arrange minimal compliance. That was the way it had always been, and that was the way they expected it to continue. A suggestion that it should be any other way was highly threatening. One of the students who had complained the loudest about history, demanding to know why they should study "a bunch of old stuff that happened thousands of years ago," averted his eyes and shrugged when asked what he thought would be a better way to use the time. "You're the teacher," he said petulantly. "You decide."

An open house planned for January gave me an opportunity to turn some of the responsibility around. I planned to have the students establish an area of study for themselves, devise a method of carrying it out, sign a contract, and then evaluate the results themselves. Towards this end I introduced a "group language/history project" to the grade tens. The only requirements were that it focus on the study of some aspect of Newfoundland society, preferably Hoberly Cove, that it utilize language skills, that there be some report or result we could exhibit at the open house, and that the work be done in groups.

When I announced this scheme in late November, everyone considered it warily, looking for the catch. It sounded too easy.

"What about grades?" someone asked suspiciously.

"You'll grade yourself individually and as a group. You know more about how hard you worked and what you got out of it than I do."

"Can it be on anything?"

"As long as it meets the requirements."

Once the initial flush wore off, the real trouble began. The class wrestled for a week without one solid proposal. Groups would form, then break up in disagreement. Finally some people began asking for suggestions, which I provided. Some began demanding assignments, which I refused. "Then I won't do anything," one boy pouted.

"Well, I can't force you. As always, what you do is up to you. But I can promise you this—that's the only way anyone will manage to fail this project."

Eventually the dissonance built to the uncomfortable point where resolution became more important than procrastination, and groups began to attack the problem. Two groups seized on an idea I had mentioned: investigating community attitudes towards certain issues, possibly via some sort of questionnaire. Despite sometimes angry pressure, however, I staunchly refused to provide topics.

Finally one group called me over. "O.K.," Frances Hodder said, "we've decided on what we're going to do." Frances was the daughter of the Salvation Army captain. "We're going to survey students' attitudes towards sex education being taught in school." I swallowed hard. O.K., I thought. You were the one advocating free inquiry and open discussion. You can't back out now. What, I wondered, will they do to me for unleashing sex education, if they nearly canned Roger for teaching evolution?

But it was clear that the project was a good one that should produce interesting data. The five group members were enthusiastic, so we drew up a short outline of the project and signed it.

And there was more to come. Another group decided on the same general idea, but they determined to look at students' and parents' attitudes towards education in Hoberly Cove. "What do you think of these questions?" one student asked. I blanched slightly as I glanced at some of their preliminary areas of concern:

religious education and sex education in the schools, how school could be improved, what should be learned in school, public exams, etc.

Other smaller groups settled on more conventional projects such as research reports, though one group wanted to put its report on a cassette and another determined to investigate the present status and future of farming in Hoberly Cove.

By Christmas, the projects were well underway. The questionnaire groups and I had developed questions (which prompted a good deal of discussion and disagreement about what constituted a good question), had run off and distributed questionnaires, and had discussed procedures for the tabulation and reporting of the data received. I looked forward to the results and braced myself for the expected repercussions.

In December, despite earlier fears to the contrary, it looked as if Jan and I were indeed going to make it to the Christmas break. And as the wet grey winter settled in more firmly, we decided that the exorbitant cost of returning to Michigan for the holidays was a bargain. We left the SAAB in Roger and Judy's care and asked them to drive us in to the airport, carrying home presents of several pairs of warm single-fingered mitts (knitted by the women in town), tins of seal meat, a pair of homemade snowshoes and two salt cod in a bag. We felt our way to the airport in a blinding blizzard, fully expecting the flight to be cancelled. But, we were assured, "We don't shut down here until it gets so thick you can't see the planes on the runway." We sprinted through the stinging snow and boarded the plane. Minutes later the pilot managed to somehow pick out the obliterated runway and put us into the air. We looked out the dark windows and watched Newfoundland disappear behind us in the snow.

7

"Should girls be allowed to take birth control pills before they are married?"

Canadians seem to have much the same opinion of Newfoundland that Americans have of Canada in general. This appears to be particularly true, for some reason, of customs and immigration officers. When we first crossed into Canada at Sarnia on our way to Hoberly Cove and applied for Landed Immigrant status, the officer there noticed that we were heading for Newfoundland. "You won't make it six months," he intoned gloomily.

"Why not?" Jan asked, her eyes wide.

"The bloody weather, the bloody people, everything."

When he saw that he was not going to deter us, however, he processed our application, muttering dour predictions under his breath.

After Christmas my father drove us back into Canada at Windsor, where we were to catch a plane to Toronto and then on to Gander. As we emerged from the tunnel and pulled up to the inspection point, the customs officer motioned us to the office, where I was ordered to fill out a declaration sheet.

I did the best I could to minimize the value of the shirts,

dresses and other gifts stuffed in our suitcases, and pushed the form across the counter to a waiting customs inspector. He snapped the form onto a clipboard and walked towards the car, with me following nervously behind. He stood by the car and studied the form intently. Finally he looked at me. "You live in Newfoundland, eh?"

"Right."

"Well, go ahead," he said. "You've got enough problems."

Doreen met us at the Gander airport in her new Datsun station wagon (which was to be subsequently pounded into junk by the roads). She had decided to come back for the time being, largely because of her local boyfriend, Ivan, but was prepared to quit teaching as soon as things began to close in again. Doreen was morose as we drove out to Hoberly Cove along the twisting road, made even narrower now by the towering piles of snow banked on each side. As she drove we tried to cheer her up, claiming that things would be better. By the time we got home, we were all feeling more confident and were able to regard the seemingly interminable winter with less trepidation.

Unfortunately, this flush of optimism was short-lived. Doreen became increasingly depressed by the school situation and resigned two weeks after returning.

I returned to school the first day back to find that a film I had ordered some months before had finally arrived. Called *No Reason to Stay*, it was a semi-autobiographical statement made by a young NFB filmmaker who had himself dropped out of school. Although Roger had seen it at the University of Toronto and recommended it highly, I was totally unprepared for the impact it was to have on the students.

I had originally brought it in primarily for the grade tens as part of our examination of the school as a social environment. The movie's theme was deceptively simple: that schools can be boring, insensitive places which frustrate originality and ignore the deeper needs of its students, and that sometimes students are left with little choice but to leave. Even though the film was in black and white and somewhat dated—the boys wore thin black ties and short hair—the movie was written and acted with such perceptiveness and honesty that it created a local sensation.

"I've never seen anything like it," one grade ten student commented in awe after I showed it the first time. "That's exactly the way it is. It didn't miss one thing."

Others were less inclined to see its absolute applicability to their situation, but all agreed that it presented a point of view seldom made with such extraordinarily effectiveness. When I showed it to my eights, they were even more overwhelmed. I showed it twice more, once in class and once at lunch, but that was still not enough. The students showed it themselves three more times after school to packed houses. Some of the kids recorded the sound track and memorized it, and for several weeks the halls reverberated with "I've Got No Reason to Stay."

Capitalizing on the enthusiasm, I put together a series of questions designed to help focus attention on the ideas presented in the film and to provide them with an opportunity to think about and write out their own feelings. One question asked them to comment on a statement made in the film: "To educate is to encourage. You do not encourage, you discourage. To educate is to interest. You do not interest, you bore." Wishing the students to move beyond a superficial reaction to the film, I asked them to describe the possible negative and positive outcomes of leaving school as the film's main character does.

The quiz was a success. The students' written and oral responses were interesting, sometimes passionate, occasionally funny. Often their criticisms and solutions were predictable and naive, but the important point was undeniable—the students were getting deeply and personally involved with their own education. We were moving away from a system of passive reception and turning it into an active process of exploration, for all of us.

Meanwhile, the grade tens were working frantically on their questionnaires. The group working on community attitudes towards education had not only passed out and collected questionnaires from virtually every high school student in Hoberly Cove but had also taken forms to more than sixty homes for the parents to complete, and had gone as well to the elementary school, where they had administered the questionnaires to the grade six classes. With all the questionnaires collected, they ended up with opinions from more than 160 students and seventy parents, not a bad sample in a town of twelve hundred. The group looking at sex education had decided to concentrate only on the attitudes of high school students, and had collected about 140 completed questionnaires.

The room looked like Gallup poll headquarters. People were dashing around picking up last-minute forms while others added up the responses and recorded them by category. Some group members figured percentages while others selected comments for inclusion. The education group decided on using a bar graph system of reporting, while the sex education people were satisfied with a percentage breakdown.

As the deadline of the open house neared, the work reached a furious pitch. The groups laboured long after school, and eventually their reports began to take form. The final drafts were ready a week before the open house, and the results were, if not startling, rather interesting. Among other findings, the "Study of Student and Parent Attitudes Towards Education in Hoberly Cove" revealed the following:

1. Percentage answering 'yes' to the question: "Do you think today's education system could be improved?

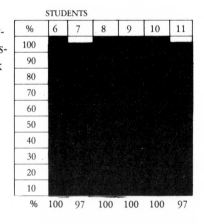

While there was general agreement between students and parents that something needed to be done, written comments and responses to the question "In what ways can it be improved?" revealed fundamentally different opinions as to what changes were called for. The students thought that the classroom was too dominated by the teacher and that there ought to be more talk and discussion, less home study, and equal privileges in such matters as smoking. Many thought that the curriculum should be more relevant to their future lives as wage earners; one specified grade nine as the point where the student might begin selecting courses that would train him for his occupation.

Opinions from the parents directly contradicted the students' views: "Not enough home studies;" "The students are getting too much freedom in class;" "[education] not as good as it was in the little school room forty years ago." Distrust of a changed or broadened curriculum was suggested in criticism of new math, sex education and school discussion of "religion." Those who attempted a helpful point of view were vague: "Many of the textbooks should be changed;" "I think the education system today is improving but there are a lot of steps to be taken yet to make it perfect." One parent grimly declared schooling "a mixture of fact and fiction, truth and mostly error."

Concerning other educational issues, most tables showed considerable agreement between students and parents.

2. Percentage answering 'yes' to the question: "Do you think you [your child] would benefit from a grade XI diploma?"

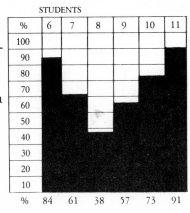

STUDENTS							PARENTS
%	6	7	8	9	10	11	
%	84	61	38	57	73	91	86

103

3. Percentage answering 'yes' to the question: "Do you think you [your child is] are learning the right things in school?"

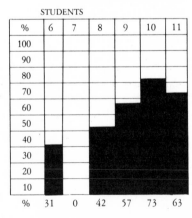

%	6	7	8	9	10	11		PARENTS
100								
90								
80								
70								
60								
50								
40								
30								
20								
10								
%	42	23	76	71	15	36		60

5. Percentage answering 'yes' to the question: "Do you think you [your children] are benefitting from home studies?"

%	6	7	8	9	10	11		PARENTS
100								
90								
80								
70								
60								
50								
40								
30								
20								
10								
%	73	78	18	14	15	63		44

8. Percentage answering 'yes' to the question: "Do you think religion should be taught in school?"

%	6	7	8	9	10	11		PARENTS
100								
90								
80								
70								
60								
50								
40								
30								
20								
10								
%	31	0	42	57	73	63		74

Significantly, in view of the other group's findings concerning sex education, this report found that sixty-seven per cent of the parents favoured the teaching of sex education in school.

The report's conclusions, however, were not models of scholarly, dispassionate summary: "As you can see, the parents' opinions did not vary a great deal from those of the students. In our opinion, the variations between the students and parents can be accounted for because the students want things changed but the parents don't." And " . . . the information we have shows us that the vast majority of the parents and students think the education system should be improved. So we think the teachers and other education authorities should try and do something about it."

The other group's report, "Students' Attitudes Towards Sex Education Being Taught In School," proved somewhat more inflammatory. The group reported its data with comments grade by grade and then tabulated the overall school results. Its major findings were that ninety-six per cent of the students thought sex should be taught in school and ninety-two wanted to know more about sex. Ninety-seven per cent said they would like to see films on sex, something they had never had. Also, the report found that sixty-five per cent wanted to know about the body and its sexual function and changes, thirty-four per cent about birth control and twenty-one per cent about abortion. The study also indicated that sixty per cent of the students polled thought that girls should be allowed to take birth control pills before marriage.

The report's recommendations were more specific and adamant. "In the future," it concluded, "we, the students, want to see sex taught as a regular class subject. We think that with 96% of the students interested in sex education there is a great need for it. If this course is not implemented a great number of students will not be as interested in the rest of their subjects, knowing that this course could be brought into their school.

"We are leaving this open to the teachers for further attention. If they want to see students more interested in school, and want to sincerely help them cope with their problems, then they should do everything they can to see sex education implemented."

Soon after we distributed the reports, saving enough to hand out to parents during open house, Norman called me aside. "Captain Hodder just called me. He wants to see you during open house."

"What about?" I asked innocently.

"About that questionnaire you did on sex education. He started in on me, but I told him I knew nothing about it, so he asked to talk to you. But since the open house was early next week, I convinced him to wait until then. You have to expect this sort of thing when you try something different, Don boy." He said it without malice or relish. Norman was a hard fellow to get a handle on. While he clearly and vocally opposed many of my ideas, he generally allowed me to do pretty much as I pleased. I could not decide if he figured I would become cynical and frustrated and fall into line, or if he got some sort of vicarious pleasure from my unconventional classroom ways. At any rate, try as I might, I could not dislike the man.

Now he was standing in front of me, warning me about what to expect. "They're really upset because their daughter was a part of the project, and I suspect Mrs. Hodder is more behind this then he is. Be ready, because they're going to put you on the spot."

The open house, other than the Hodders' visit, was something of an anticlimax. It was primarily a social evening with coffee and gossip, one of the few opportunities for the town to congregate. I enjoyed meeting the parents, but generally they were content to shake my hand, pick up the reports, glance at the model of agricultural use in Hoberly Cove, pick up a booklet of poetry turned out by another group and, smiling all the while, circulate out of the room. A few asked about grades, but they accepted whatever marks or work samples I offered with the same smiling equanimity. I sensed that, to them, it was unthinkable to contradict or even question the mysterious grading formula understood only by those initiated into the teaching fraternity.

The Hodders, however, were different. They came into my room, then empty, shortly before we were to close up. As they entered, both dressed in their severe black and red Salvation Army uniforms, Captain Hodder closed the door behind him ominously. Mrs. Hodder ("How do you address her?" I wondered. "Mrs. Captain? Captain? Mrs.?") sat primly in a chair in front of my desk, her hair pulled back from her face and stuffed into a bonnet. Her husband sat next to her, his hat grasped firmly in his hands. The motto on the badge, I noticed, was "Blood and Fire."

Captain Hodder's stern voice broke the quiet of the room. "Mr. Sawyer, we would like to talk to you about the sex education survey Frances has been doing in your class."

"Yes," I beamed, "quite interesting, isn't it?"

Mrs. Hodder's lips, drawn into a thin line, barely moved. "Do you feel this is the sort of thing our children should be doing in school?"

"Well, yeah, as a matter of fact I think it's exactly the sort of thing we should be doing in school. This is inductive learning at its best. These kids came up with a question, developed a program for exploring that question, then carried through on it beautifully. They wrote the questions, presented the questionnaires, worked together to tabulate the results and put together a report of completely primary data. I think it's quite exciting."

Mrs. Hodder did not look excited at all. "But why, Mr. Sawyer, did you feel it necessary to assign this particular topic? Wouldn't any question have provided the same opportunities?"

"Mrs. Hodder, I didn't assign this topic. They chose it entirely on their own."

"I don't believe for a minute that you did not suggest this," she retorted belligerently. "I don't think these children would have decided on this topic by themselves."

I tried to remain calm. "Don't sell these kids short. I assure you that outside of suggesting the general idea of a questionnaire, I had nothing to do with their choice of subject. They're quite capable of thinking for themselves."

"Mr. Sawyer," Captain Hodder broke in. "We were particularly upset by this question: 'Do you think girls should be allowed to take birth control pills before marriage?' Now this is entirely a moral question, and the teaching of morals has no place in the classroom."

I avoided debating that issue. "The question asks students to

107

give their opinion based on their system of values, Captain Hodder," I said, "but neither I nor anyone else tried to imply that one response was correct or another wrong." That, I suspected, was the problem.

Mrs. Hodder was not placated. "Bringing up this sort of thing can lead to promiscuity. You're condoning these attitudes."

"You don't seem to understand," I said in exasperation. "I didn't design the project, make up or answer the questions, or even give my opinion. I'm not condoning or condemning anything. All your daughter and the rest of her group did was identify an issue that was important to them and then find out how other students felt about it. And I think that their results indicate that many students share their concern. That's the whole point of a survey like this. And don't forget that this problem is very real to these kids. Not only are many of them going through some difficult physical and emotional changes, with all too often no place to turn for help, but the results of ignoring the situation can be tragic. Did you know three girls dropped out of school last year in grades eight, nine and ten because of pregnancy? And two girls have dropped out of high school already this year. One girl dropped out of fifth grade two years ago, and apparently she didn't even know how she got pregnant. Pretending that sexuality will go away if we ignore it just doesn't work."

Though my voice had risen somewhat as I got more involved with my explanation, the effect seemed to be a calming one, as the Hodders skirted further discussion of the topic. Instead, we talked briefly about their daughter's grades and behaviour, both of which suffered considerably, I felt, from the tension she apparently felt as a result of their expectations of what she should be and think. I tried to tactfully avoid verbalizing this suspicion outright and only hinted at my feelings, but the couple soon decided they had heard enough, nodded a stiff good night and walked into the now deserted hall. Though I felt things had gone fairly well, I wondered how much they had heard of what I had said.

I picked up my stack of books and papers with a sigh, flicked off the lights in my room and emerged to find that only Simon

Fillier, the maintenance man, and I remained in the school. Simon and his wife kept both the elementary school and high school clean, and usually worked far into the night.

"Looks like the weather might get a little rough tonight, Mr. Sawyer." Simon looked brightly up at me above his glasses. "We must have three or four inches of snow already and it's coming down thicker all the time. With the wind picking up the way it is, I wouldn't be surprised if we lost the electricity again."

The power lines to Hoberly Cove ran from Northport for thirty miles along the exposed shores of Hamilton Sound: already we had lost the power once for half a day during an earlier winter storm, when the wind had knocked out a section of line. Apparently, however, such outages normally occurred with considerable frequency and, depending on the severity of the weather, for much longer periods.

I said good night to Simon and walked out into the growing storm. I had been so intent on the discussions inside that I had failed to notice that the snow, which had started falling lightly in the afternoon, had turned into a blizzard. The wind had risen and was now pushing the snowflakes horizontally so that they struck me squarely in the eyes as I tried to claw my way to the car. Despite the deepening snow, my snow tires, which were just a little too big and kept grating on the front fenders when I turned, managed to pull me onto the road. Visibility was almost nil; I had to grope blindly through the snow towards our apartment, hoping that I was still on the road.

Eventually I struggled into the garden and shut off the car. I was almost blown through the front door, where May was waiting, wringing her hands. "Oh, Mr. Don. I'm some glad you're home," she said. "This is no night to be out."

Jan was making charts and games—she had had to make almost all the materials she needed for her class—but looked up excitedly as I came in. "Isn't this great? Let's take a walk!"

"A walk? You can hardly stand up out there, and the temperature is near zero."

"Oh, come on. It'll be fun. I've never been out in a storm like this."

No amount of persuasion could convince her that storms were things people avoided, not sought out. I sat down and had a beer to fortify myself for the ordeal, listening all the while to the shrieking of the wind. Working from the feet up, we applied layer after layer of wool and flannel to our bodies in preparation for what I hoped would be a very short foray into the howling storm.

By the time we were sufficiently garbed for the storm, we were both only semi-ambulatory: to walk, we pivoted from one stiff leg to the other like primitive robots. But when we opened the door and plunged into the biting wind, we were grateful for every thread we had buttoned, laced, buckled or tied to our bodies.

The night was so black that even the snowflakes that flew in our faces were dark and glimmerless. The wind rushed from the invisible sea with ferocity and our ears became so filled with its sharp rising and falling crescendo that we could not even shout to each other and be heard. Jan motioned out the gate and I followed, leaning hard into the icy blasts that whined around the low sheds on the waterfront. We slowly made our way onto the road, now obliterated by deep drifts of snow as well as utter darkness, and struggled onto the lane that led up the hill to the ridge. Going away from the water was easier, as the wind pushed us firmly on the back. Only the swirling drifts that extended long, heavy fingers across the road hindered our progress. We picked our way upward largely by the porch lights which lined the lane.

As we shivered in our shirts, sweaters, coats, scarves and caps, Jan tried to shout something over the wind. I shook my head that I could not understand. She pointed into the darkness at a house on our right. There, emerging onto the open porch from the brightly illuminated kitchen, was a grey-haired man wearing only wool socks, a pair of pants and a sleeveless T shirt. He stalked unhesitatingly out into the porch, closed the door behind him, rested his hands on the railing and gazed deeply into the gale that screamed furiously around his exposed shoulders. We continued, and the man remained standing unconcernedly on the porch until he was obscured by the snow and darkness.

We made it up to the high road and began the journey back,

only to find what I had feared—that the trip back down was immensely more difficult than going up. We could hardly move at all directly into the wind, so, holding hands to avoid being separated, we began tacking a zig-zag course down the hill, our heads lowered into the teeth of the mounting gale. The distance was only about half a mile, but we were nearly exhausted before we were half way. The drifts were constantly shifting and growing, and we often blundered blindly into them, tripping and falling heavily into the snow. The inky blackness, the numbing cold and the deafening howl of the wind contributed to our growing panic.

Somehow we struggled to the lower road and almost crawled through the drifts that separated us from the garden entrance. Once there, we merely stood up and let the wind blow us, stumbling and clutching each other, to the Pikes' front door. I managed to get to the door knob but my frozen fingers could hardly manipulate the handle. As I struggled to pull the door open against the wind, Carl threw open the inner door, nudged open the storm door and scooped us into their warm, deafeningly quiet foyer.

Though May clucked reprovingly as she fed us hot tea and wrapped us in blankets, we must have looked so thoroughly miserable and penitent that she didn't have the heart to say anything to us about our foolhardiness. Carl just looked grave and shook his head. "I'm glad I didn't know you were out there," he said. "I'd have been worried sick. A winter storm is nothing to provoke. Many good men and women have died in storms no worse than this, only a few hundred yards from their doorstep."

Shivering, we crawled under the covers on our bed and fell instantly asleep.

The next morning I awoke with my knees pulled up to my chest, still shivering. I was tangled up with Jan and we were wound up tightly in the covers like twin moths. Someone was tapping gently at the door to our apartment.

"Mr. Don," May called. "Mr. Don."

I emerged from my stupor enough to answer groggily. "Yes, May. What is it?"

"You and Jan had better get up at once, Mr. Don. The power

went off in the night and we're all going up to Alpheaus and Nancy's because they have a wood stove. You come along or you'll die from the cold."

Huddled and trembling in the bed, I was not at all sure she was exaggerating. I shook Jan awake and we fumbled our way into the warmest dry clothes we could find, shivering uncontrollably.

May was waiting in the hall bundled from head to toe and carrying a basket of bread and tarts. She led us out the door and into the aftermath of the storm. The sky was lifting and the sun began to shine coldly on towering heaps of snow. Carl had already dug his way out of the house and as we passed through the door we walked between sheer white walls cut into a sloping drift that reached five feet up the side of the house. Only occasional gusts of swirling snow remained to remind us of the violent winds that had battered us the night before.

As far as we could see, drifts lay high against houses and sheds, often extending across the roads in impenetrable barriers ten feet thick and six feet high. Yet despite the enormous mounds of sculpted snow piled against fences and across the roads, there were occasional dark patches of bare ground swept clean by the wind.

The Pikes had gathered in the basement of Alpheaus and Nancy's home and were clustered around the old pot-bellied stove that Alpheaus had kept mainly as a fireplace. But it still served its original function well, and the basement was warm and bright. It was obvious that all were enjoying themselves and were not anxious to see the power flick on too soon, ruining the enchantment of the crackling fire and the ease that comes of knowing there is nothing to be done.

As nostalgic stories were told of old times long before electricity came into the village, I commented that in some ways it was too bad those times were gone, and that perhaps a high price had been paid for the convenience of oil furnaces and electric lights.

"Oh, I wouldn't say that, Don," Alpheaus said thoughtfully, "not at all. You'd have to live through it to understand."

"That's right," Carl agreed. "We speak fondly of those times, and there's not a man in town who doesn't miss them sometimes. But there's also not a person in town who's been through them that would go back."

"No, Don boy," Alpheaus mused, "those were hard times. People died needlessly and suffered constantly. We talk about the good parts, but we also remember the bad times."

In the early afternoon the sky had cleared to a pale blue, and the sun gleamed blindingly off the snow that still spread over the town. The night before I had been made aware of the inadequacy of my old leather boots and, since we had got word that the school would not be open until the next afternoon at the earliest, I decided to walk over to Abner Pritchett's store and buy a new pair of insulated rubber boots.

Though he lived modestly and usually wore the scruffiest clothes imaginable, Abner was widely reputed to be a millionaire. He had inherited the store, and his money, from his father, who had reportedly gouged the community for several decades and amassed a fortune in the process. Until the coming of the fishermen's union and the Co-op store, the few merchants in town, especially Abner's father, since he had the only adequate loading dock, had a virtual stranglehold on the town. Like the fish merchants who named the price at which they would buy fish, knowing that the fisherman had no alternative but to sell at whatever rate they established, so the merchants could charge almost whatever prices they liked in the villages. And as the winter wore on and supplies dwindled, the merchants would often inflate their prices, reaping enormous profits.

Traditionally, the townspeople had had little recourse. They often combined to buy their basic supplies co-operatively, as Carl had told us, but many incidental and emergency supplies still had to be bought from the storekeepers. Their only revenge was simple but devastating: social ostracism. The merchants were often regarded as pariahs and forced to live largely outside of the sustaining social organization of the community. The people might have to buy from them, but they did not have to invite them into their homes or otherwise socialize with them.

Some of this taint seemed to linger, but the times had changed as the town gained access to supermarkets in Gander and as many new shops, now easily supplied, grew up in town. Abner, an intense, hook-nosed man aged somewhere between fifty and seventy, was no longer resented but was now regarded as something of an eccentric. Surprisingly, he was active in community affairs and was as shrewd as anyone in town. He seemed to operate his store almost as a hobby, and it remained a preposterous, impractical institution from another era.

To say that it was a general store would not sufficiently describe the scope or extent of its offerings. Walking in the front door was like walking back a hundred years. Aluminum and enamelled pots hung from wires stretched between the walls and old wood display cases arranged in a broken U around the dingy interior were full of dusty clocks, skeins of wool and ribbon, handkerchiefs and hundreds of other small items. Shelves lined the walls from floor to ceiling and were stocked with dozens of ancient patent medicines, canned goods, tea and cigarettes. In a room off to one side were kept stacks of overalls, dresses, jeans, coats and boxes of shoes and boots of indeterminable age. A large old wood stove sat solidly in the middle of the main room, its pipe making a curve and running through a hole in one wall. From the pipe dropped wires for hanging up patrons' and visitors' wet mitts. The place smelled dusty and old, with a touch of wood smoke and wet wool.

The store itself was fascinating enough; the second floor—the "storage room"—was even more so. The entire area, an enormous room half the size of our school auditorium, was jammed with a huge collection of heaped boxes and obscure items. In one corner I found a dozen oil lanterns, at least twenty years old, that had never been used, and under a table there was a box full of wooden forms for making shoes. Against a wall was a bag of rusting horseshoe nails. Harnesses for horses hung from pegs, and dust-covered boxes yielded boots that were stylish in the '20s and tools some people would consider antiques. Crockery jugs and porcelain wash basins were stacked at random.

This day, however, I just wanted a pair of boots. And, though Abner always gave me the feeling I was being taken, his prices were actually no worse than anyone else's in town. When I walked in, a group of men were already clustered around the stove, discussing the storm and smoking their pipes. I listened politely for a few moments, then during a lull in conversation asked Abner to show me his boots. I found a pair that were warm, waterproof and well fitting and was paying him when Norman walked in the store.

"Now boys," he reported breathlessly, "we've got a little job for you. The storm blew over a couple of the boats by the landing; Jim Fillier's boat slid almost down to the water, and we've got to help pull them back up."

Abner stayed in his store, but the rest of us, about six men, walked a half mile to the skidway where half a dozen boats had been hauled onto shore and blocked for the winter. Five or six more men, a couple of them my students, were already by the boats. Several boats were on their sides and one had slid so far that its bow almost touched the floating ice that covered the harbour.

"Wind hit ninety miles an hour at Cape Freels last night before the wind gauge broke," I heard one say.

Another man nodded assent. "They say it could have gotten over a hundred miles an hour."

"Well, boys," Norman said. "That boat isn't coming up by itself."

The whole group walked down to the boat at the foot of the ramp. I looked at Norman in disbelief. The boat was at least twenty-five feet long and with its heavy spruce planking must have weighed several tons. Because the electric winch was not working, apparently the twelve of us were supposed to pull it twenty yards up the ramp to its original berth. I did not see how it could be done. Still, no one else seemed daunted, so I grabbed the gunwale and waited.

"All right," one man said. "Ready? Here we go."

"All haul, boys, HAUL!" he began, everyone joining the chant. When the final word was shouted, we all pulled in a single motion and, to my amazement, the boat nudged up the slope.

"All haul, boys, HAUL!" we chanted again, and again the boat slid slowly but perceptibly upward. Each time we yelled

115

"HAUL!" I thrust hard with my legs against the slats of the ramp and felt the boat move almost easily another few feet. In fifteen minutes we had her at the original site, blocked and secure again. I looked around at the other men, beaming like mad; I felt like a member of a football team that had just won the conference championship.

We soon righted the other boats and re-blocked them. I was about to head back to Alpheaus's when Norman, chuckling out of sheer pleasure, said: "Come on back to Abner's for a few minutes, Don, then we'll walk up to Morgan's and have a few beers. What do you say?"

Several of us walked back to Abner's, kicking the snow off our boots as we entered and hanging our wet mitts by the stove.

"Abner, boy," Norman said delightedly, "that was one bloody awful storm we had last night. I can't remember when boats were knocked around like that."

Abner looked down his long, curved nose disdainfully. "That little blow? Go on. Why, I remember the time. . . "

8

"We have to change,
for survival"

From the beginning of the school year, I had laid heavy emphasis on creative writing in my English classes, not only because it allowed me to use props and approaches that made English more fun but also because I felt it provided the best opportunity to develop in the students a respect for their own writing. For most, this aim had been achieved; after the first step of believing that they could write something they became aware that they could write adequately and finally realized that they could write better. As the year progressed, so did the writing. Vague generalities and abstractions slowly gave way to preciseness. The kids' writings began to exhibit their innate sense of language and image; it reflected their world with the same clarity and brilliance with which they perceived it.

I had originally planned to proceed in a series of fluid steps to poetry, where I hoped the students would be able to further sharpen their developing descriptive tools. Along the way, however, we got sidetracked by play writing. Though the skits they wrote relied on gag humour and slapstick, the enthusiasm with which they collaborated on their scripts, the prodigiousness of their output and the obvious joy they derived from acting more than made up for any lapses in quality. Particularly startling to me was the willingness, even eagerness, of every person to participate. At times I had despaired of ever seeing all the kids actively involved in class. Some of them, especially a few of the grade eight girls, had seemed painfully withdrawn, even though their writing suggested that they were quietly participating.

Initially I had tried to deal with the situation by discussing it. Many of the kids, especially some of the boys, had learned to bolster their own competitive situation and ego by ridiculing classmates. Talking this out opened up the larger area of sexual and social roles. But in the end the most effective way of involving the quiet ones was by fully and uncritically accepting their nonverbal participation and allowing them to work slowly into activities. Now, to my astonishment, people who usually contributed less than a spoken sentence a day in class were taking the stage without persuasion and spouting line after line to the audience, even the whole school, with feeling. They had a role to hide behind, and the shield of the character made them less vulnerable to criticism or self-doubt.

The major result was a broader, keener interest in and contribution to the class activity on the part of those who had formerly withheld their involvement. The increased ease and confidence they gained through acting, and the new respect they developed both for themselves and each other were transferred to other areas as well.

Eventually I introduced the idea of moving into poetry, and the response was predictable—groans could be heard throughout the school. Maxwell Parsons actually held his stomach in pain. "By jeez, Sawyer"—we had become less formal since the beginning of the year—"you said English was going to be fun. I hate old poetry more than a toothache." His face was contorted in genuine agony.

But they had never written poetry before. Poetry was the slow, numbing dissection of classics word by word, beat by beat. I hoped to present it as their own language, their own imagination expressed in verse. I tried to emphasize that poetry was the freest form of expression, and could be largely unencumbered by the restrictions of grammar and punctuation. But they were not con-

118

vinced. Even the free-form work of Lawrence Ferlinghetti, Kenneth Patchen and e.e. cummings failed to make an impression. I could change the content, but this subtlety was lost—to them the game was the same. Early attempts at original poetry were dismally rhymed, nonsensical imitations of what they thought I thought poetry was. Even prohibiting rhyme and taking their own excellent descriptive prose and reworking it into verse did not work.

I ended up resorting to the sometimes overworked haiku. To them it was something new. Not only had they never written haiku, they had never even read any. I wrote a simple introduction to the form with some examples, and our study of poetry began in earnest.

That sheet was the last non-student poetry I used that year, in English 8 or 10. Fascinated and unintimidated by the simple yet intricate poems I gave them, the students began a torrent of original haikus. Many kids, finding tremendous gratification in seizing a thought and working it into a short, finished form, would hand in fifteen or twenty poems at a time. Moreover, many of the students who still felt incapable of good expository writing seemed to excel at haiku, demonstrating to me and themselves that they did indeed possess creativity and the ability to express themselves effectively.

I was so impressed by the first batch of haiku from my tens that I stencilled off a dozen without the names of the writers and distributed them to the class. Everyone read the poems quietly, but once in a while I would catch someone flashing me a quick look on coming across a poem he or she had written. Finally Jeff Fillier looked up. "Who wrote these?"

"A group of poets, Jeff. What do you think of them?"

"They're good," he said certainly. "Real good."

"Would you believe me if I told you that they were all written by people in our class?"

Jeff laughed. "No."

"Well, they were."

"They couldn't have been. Nobody in here can write like this."

After much discussion, and after other students took credit

for some of the poems, he finally believed me. But the class was genuinely awed. Two things contributed to the class's disbelief: first, they had never really seen and considered the quality of their own work; second, their own work had never been used as literature, as writing worthy of serious regard and study. If it had been used at all, it was generally viewed as inadequate or incomplete; not as whole, effective writing. The effects of this new perspective were dramatic. On the writing level, the students were encouraged and excited by their rediscovered capabilities, and they wrote with even finer sensitivity and construction. More important was the new regard they had for their classmates.

Many of the haikus the students wrote depended on the traditional drawing of relationships between seemingly unrelated subjects for their effectiveness.

> Like wind-swayed flowers
> They walk the streets together
> Three drunken people

> It stroked my chilled flesh
> Like the hands of a lover
> Dawn light of the morn

> A stubbly brown quilt
> Patchwork of dirty white snow
> Early spring meadow

Others drew directly on their perceptions of their surroundings, but expressed them in imagery that was original and often unexpected.

> Flowerless garden
> In summer a senseless smell
> Only fading grass

> Green and white classroom
> Full of solitude and fear
> Like a bleak dungeon

> The icicles cried
> As the warm sunshine kissed
> Cold weather goodbye

But soon poems started arriving that did not fit into the haiku
format:

Dark gloomy shadows, creeping slowly
through rotten wood, fear growing in the centre
of old trees. Cold and white things turn.
Frost has come to every living thing.

These grew into longer poems, and finally came right around
to the traditional poetic form of the community—the ballad.

The Ballad of the Red Dumptruck
I'd like to live in Vancouver, West coast sunny shore
But there is something here in Hoberly that I like even more
And the thing that I might get, and all I need is a little
luck,
is to sit behind the wheel of the Council's red dump truck.
How nice to be in that big G.M.
the motor with power to spare
And the new ones won't be out
for at least another year.
You take a load of gravel
to be spreaded over the hill
you just sit there smiling
looking through the big windshield
That great big dump there on the rear
is a thousand pounds or more
them great big double headlights and
the split shift on the floor.
The clearance lights and safety glass—a man must feel so
free
Blowing for the open road in the Council's G.M.C.
The man who's got a job on it, he's got to take a test
Beaton Abbot's got the contract to keep the tires the very
best.
The rubber must be perfect
so it won't get stumped
Because there are no rebuilt parts
for the council's red dump truck
Bill Whiteway is the driver, he's been driving it a year
Oh how happy I'll be when he quits his job

121

and goes back to Bay de Spear
But it's only then I'll get the chance
to really change my luck
And to sit behind the wheel
of the Council's red dump truck.

A certain sign that the kids were now relaxed enough to enjoy
writing was that some of the poems demonstrated the wit so evident outside of school but hitherto banned inside. Not wanting
to antagonize the Hodders any more than necessary, I refrained
from handing out copies of one eighth-grade student's poem and
only read it aloud in class:

Abner Pritchett's Paint
Abner, boy, I got complaint
About one can of ten-cent paint
My wife, she buy in your damn store
And now, by Christ, I'm pretty sore.

You see, last week the spring it come
And everything was on the bum
The walls and floors, the windows too,
It was dirty as hell, I'm telling you.

My wife she's clean and she is neat
So she bought paint for toilet seat
And one whole week we watch with eye
But damn paint it not get dry.

I say to wife, it serves you right
You try to be so money tight
That ten-cent paint, it no damn good
It won't get dry on no damn wood.

My daughter, too, get ring around
When on toilet she sat down
For one whole week we stand and wait
And now we all got complaint.

Abner, boy, we don't know what to do
We got to eat and let some come through
When pains come and I almost faint
and squirm and think of that damn paint.

My wife got a sister named Marie
she lives all the time in house with me
You know how sexy she raises her head
I sneak sometime in Marie's bed

Last night I look where she sit down
And there she too got white ring around
And now off the tail of Marie
I got white ring on front of me

Now, Mr. Abner, I ask you
Just what in hell we going to do?
How can our home be nice and neat
If paint no dry on damn toilet seat?

I decided to make student writing our primary material as much as possible, and, when spring finally began to nudge out the seemingly endless winter and we were able to get out again, I had an opportunity to try the approach in my History 10 class. I had wanted to shift our focus from the school and from national and international events to the community itself, but had been rebuffed by the weather. In April, spring seemed to have begun a fretful advance, and I decided to seize the next decent day to visit the four or five major graveyards in town.

"Graveyards? Why should we go there?"

"Because we're trying to construct a sketch of the community's history, right?"

"Well, yeah."

"And where can you go to find more local history than into the graveyards?"

The consensus seemed to be that there were several places, but by the time we figured out what could be obtained from gravestones—names of early families, average life expectancy during different periods, time and origins of first settlement, causes of death, incidence of epidemics and child mortality, religious and philosophical views, etc.—the class seemed interested, even eager.

I explained how to make rubbings of gravestones, and we

formed five groups, one group per graveyard. Each group was to bring back rubbings of its favourite stones, and compile and mimeograph a report on its graveyard, including the average age of death, the main causes of death, the oldest stone and any other information the group members could glean which they felt would be helpful. At the class's request, I agreed to write up my own report as well. I also suggested that the kids talk to their parents or other elders in the community about any questions the information raised.

We combined the results of the study into a twelve-page booklet, and the findings were as interesting as I had hoped. The overall average age of death worked out to be thirty-four, a remarkable statement about the dangers and privation of life in early Hoberly Cove. Also, the incidence of infant mortality was staggering. Kay Pearce found out from her grandparents that there had been an outbreak of typhoid fever in 1917, which explained why there seemed to be clusters of deaths around this date. Some of the kids also found out that tuberculosis was the worst killer of young people. The frequency of death among the young impressed many of them deeply. "At that time," one group wrote, "I don't think people took it so hard when a young person died as they would now. Now we find it very hard to forget, whereas at that time it was so common, it was forgotten almost as soon as it happened—except for the relatives." Another group made up mostly of young women made an interesting observation that had escaped the rest of us: "We also noticed the inscriptions on many stones referred to young brides and their babies, which probably means they died in childbirth and that the infants died, too."

We found several deaths by drowning, and the epitaph on the stone of one victim, who drowned on Christmas Day 1875, left a chilling view of life and death during this period:

Death rides on every breeze;
He lurks in every flower;
Each season has its own disease,
Its perils every hour.

As a way of leading into a study of the community, the project had been a success. But just as important from my point of view was the fact that once again student-generated material was providing the "text." We used the information compiled by the groups for further investigation and as the basis of class discussion; their ideas and work, not the product of anonymous historians, was at the heart of our study. By this time the class had begun to see this situation as natural, and the time and thoughtfulness reflected in some of the reports showed not only that they recognized their expanding role but also that they accepted the increased responsibility that went along with it.

Some of the teachers had a much harder time accepting the shift in responsibility that I was labouring to execute. When I had distributed copies of the modest stencilled handwritten report on the graveyards, I had not expected much reaction one way or another. For Calvin, however, the report provided an opportunity to release some of his frustration with me and my ideas that had begun with our dispute over grading and that had been building over the past months.

Our sharpest conflict had occurred a few months before over a seemingly innocuous snowball fight. One afternoon, before we had been given keys to the school, Roger and I had arrived at school to find it locked. More and more kids drifted to school, and, with snow on the ground and time on our hands, before long Roger and I and a few allies had accepted a good-natured challenge and were battling a massed army of noticeably more accurate students. Badly outnumbered, we retreated to the parking lot, where we were holding our own when Norman and Calvin drove up. Norman was clearly off limits and made it to the door unscathed, but Calvin, who was feared by many of the students because of his severe classroom personality, was thumped on the back by an anonymous hurler as he turned to enter the door.

The incident did not even register at the time; Roger and I had more important things to worry about, such as how to run the blockade without being thoroughly pelted. The attackers clobbered us both as we dashed to safety, and once inside, Roger and I made our way, laughing, to the staff room. Suddenly Calvin burst out of the staff room door and slammed into a student who had been walking towards his room, knocking the boy through an open door into the seats. Shocked, we ran into the classroom. The boy was crying, but not seriously hurt.

But that was not the end of it. Norman called us in to the staff room before classes began. He rebuked us as well as the students.

"You all know what happened today," he began earnestly. "Well, I'm not prepared to let these kids get away with this sort of thing." He was beginning to get worked up now. "Some of you may choose to let your students throw snowballs at you," he glared at me and Roger. "But as long as I'm principal here, I'll continue to demand respect for my teachers. I want to find the student who hit Calvin with a snowball, and I'm holding the entire school in this afternoon until the person who threw it comes forward and apologizes. Then he'll be punished."

"If anybody should apologize," I said, "it's Calvin." Calvin, who was in the staff room too, was furious. He said nothing, but glowered at me, and I stared back with equal intensity. Norman quickly saw that the situation was on the verge of exploding. "Now let's get to our classes," he said hurriedly, "and we'll hold our students after school and talk to them about this incident."

"My students are leaving at three-ten, Norman," I gritted out. "And if you want to bring this to the board I'll be happy to take it up there." I snatched my books off the counter and stalked to my room.

Kids have an extraordinary talent for knowing exactly what is happening at all times. Before I had managed to sit down they began asking me if the school would be kept in and what would happen to the culprit who had hit Calvin. Under the circumstances, and given my feelings, I decided not to discuss the issue in class. But at ten past three, when the bell rang ending school, the class looked at me expectantly. The rest of the school was as quiet as a tomb. "You're dismissed," I said quietly. As soon as they opened the door, Roger's class left their room, quickly followed by the rest of the classes. Except for Calvin's, that is. That unfortunate group was kept in for an hour while he ranted. But that afternoon ended the incident, and nothing more was said about it.

Nonetheless, Calvin's resentment continued. Ironically though, I basically liked Calvin, and, I think, he liked me. He was a bright, intellectually capable man. We spent hours discussing educational and political philosophy in the pub; over beers our arguing was free of rancour and more likely to be punctuated by laughs and smiles than shouts. But in school he was a different man. He felt the need to maintain a silent, tightly ordered classroom which never threatened his unquestioned and absolute authority. My approach was and continued to be an affront to everything he believed about school and the role of the teacher. And unfortunately the school's inherent inflexibility, which worked against an acceptance of differences among educators as well as students, forced us into increasingly antagonistic stances; there was no opportunity for us to coexist.

So in school we generally tried to stay out of each other's way and usually avoided critical remarks about each other. Occasionally, however, an incident like the snowball fight would arise which would provoke one of us, and we would find ourselves locked in conflict again. Though I certainly had not expected it, our graveyard report proved to be such an issue by launching a debate on, of all things, local dialect.

"Don," Calvin said as he leafed through the paper. "I don't see how you can let some of these errors go. Some of the English in here is terrible."

In actuality most of it was not bad at all. "Look, Calvin, every kid in that class contributed something. Of course it's going to be of mixed quality. But overall I think it's pretty well done. I looked at it fairly closely and didn't notice any particularly glaring errors, and the ones that were made we went over in class. People can learn a lot from mistakes, but they have to write enough to make them first."

"Look at this now." He pointed to a concluding statement in one of the reports. "'Some died for an instance of drowning and more died accidently'," he read mockingly. "Not very well worded, I'd say."

"But that was written by two guys who hardly wrote anything at the beginning of the year," I protested. "I pointed out to them the right way to use 'for instance' and the function of commas in a sentence, and I think they'll be better able to avoid those problems in the future."

"Well, what about the way they use 'more'?"

"That's mostly a dialectal thing, Calvin. You know that's common. 'More' is often used for 'some' here."

"Maybe so, but it's not correct. You know you can't let these kids write and speak incorrectly just because that's the way they've grown up. Let them get to Toronto and they'll find out soon enough that talking like a Newfie makes people look on you as a fool and costs you jobs."

Norman had been listening interestedly. "I agree. There's nothing at all to this dialect stuff. These students have to learn the way they speak in the rest of Canada if they're ever going to make it away from home. I know. I ended up fighting more than working in Toronto because of my accent, and there are not many employers who look beyond your speech."

I was surprised by the strength of their feelings. "I can appreciate what you're saying, but in my opinion you have to begin language training by first convincing the student that he can communicate effectively, and you're not going to do that by correcting him every time he lapses into the language that surrounds him in his home and his community. We have to accept the language he brings into school with him as a deep part of the individual. If we start immediately trying to cut that out of him, he's going to end up withdrawn and confused. And my experience has been that having confidence in yourself is the most critical prerequisite for getting and holding a job, as well as being happy with yourself."

"That's easy for you to say," Willis added, "you've always spoken regular English. For us it's a different matter. We have to change for survival."

I began to feel defensive. "Look, first of all we're talking about a dialect, a form of English. If people are prejudiced against those who speak non-standard dialects, the problem lies with them." I knew that was a weak argument, but I thought it had to be made. "Also, in Newfoundland, the standard dialect is not

CBC English. If we're turning out people for Toronto, then let's root out all the traditional values and patterns and make everyone think and talk the same. But if we're supposedly equipping people to deal with the life and problems of Hoberly Cove or even of Newfoundland, we're not going to do that by making them ashamed of the way they and their parents speak."

"Don," Norman pointed out, "it's our problem, because they are the people who control jobs and money. We have to conform to them, not them to us. I can speak two languages—with the boys and with teachers. I had to learn both to survive. Don't you correct them when they make a mistake?"

"It depends, on the person and the slip," I hedged. "But from the beginning I told my students that, in the context of their community, it was they who were speaking standard English and I who was speaking a non-standard dialect. They're exposed to a midwestern United States version of standard English every time I open my mouth. And they learn again and again that other people don't speak like they do whenever they flip on the TV or radio. They know it all too well, but to make them even more self-conscious about their speech patterns by attacking them in school is, in my opinion, destructive in the long run. I think that if they develop the confidence and basic language skills necessary to express themselves effectively, the dialect will take care of itself; they'll be able to adjust quickly to standard English when and if it is necessary."

Despite the very real importance of the dialectal question, which simmered uneasily as long as we were there, more immediate challenges had to be met daily in the classroom. I was learning quickly that traditional study material could be used effectively, often by merely changing its emphasis or treatment. This was the case with several novels, such as *Lost Horizon*, which allowed us to engage in far-ranging discussions on the future, religion, values, culture, and what it was that made life meaningful, as well as geography and history. We ended work on the novel, which saw everyone reading individually at his own pace, with yet another Deep Thought Quiz that tried to help the stu-

129

dents to focus in on their feelings about the subjects we had broached and to imagine how the characters in the novel would relate to their own setting of Hoberly Cove. They were asked to develop any three of these scenes: Conway walks into Abner Pritchett's store and asks for a pack of cigarettes; Mallinson's car veers off the road and he walks up to Morgan Pearce's garage to get help; Barnard is stranded for a day when his car breaks down; Miss Brinklow comes to the school as an inspector for the Denominational Education Commission.

By now an area that caused me more concern than English was the teaching of Newfoundland geography in grade eight. We had spent over six months working on many different approaches to the land and culture of Africa, and the classes had gone extremely well. Nonetheless, we eventually ran out of ideas and interest and still had three months to work with. I rejected the idea of shifting to another "southern land." We had acquired the skills and concepts of mapping, political entities, the interrelationship between culture and environment, racial adaptation and racial conflict, colonialism, etc. through our exhaustive African study, and so we decided to end up as I had originally planned—looking, quite literally, at the geography of Newfoundland.

The slim text available, about forty pages, took a hard line on geography. Essentially it addressed itself to two things: glaciers and rocks. I had absolutely no background whatsoever in either, and consequently I was somewhat apprehensive about plunging into it in class. So, while we waited for the weather to warm and the rocks to thaw, we discussed the continental drift theory, which no one had ever heard of, and considered the size and effects of the glaciers that had gouged and re-gouged Newfoundland as recently as ten thousand years before.

But eventually we started on the formation and identification of rocks, with me learning right along with everyone else. One morning Kevin, Terry Rowe and Warrick came rushing into class to report their discovery of a fossil bird on the "tower"—a low rocky rise that happened to be the highest point in the vicinity.

To substantiate their claim, they had brought in a chunk of stone that was a maze of branch-like formations. "This is the nest, you see," Terry said. They insisted that I accompany them in an expedition that afternoon after school.

I was home about 4:00 waiting for them to appear for our trip when a knock came at the door. Before I could answer—we had had a hard enough time persuading people to knock first—the three traipsed into the kitchen. "Look who's here," Kevin announced. "Warrick, who swore he'd never set foot in any teacher's house."

Warrick looked sheepishly at the floor and I wanted to change the subject before he bolted and ran. Before I could say anything, Terry, who had been over often, continued tormenting Warrick. "I thought you said you wished every teacher would burn forever in the flames of hottest hell, Warrick boy." Warrick shuffled his feet uneasily. "And that you'd sooner die than set one foot in a house where one lived."

I collected our gear as quickly as possible before Warrick decided that the best way out of the contradiction was to leave and never return. We had decided to take a Polaroid camera and a hammer in order to send a picture of the bird and a sample of the rock to the geology department at Memorial University in St. John's. We drove up the hill and to the abrupt end of a rough lane that ran between small gardens. We then took a trail that wound through scrub aspen, which was just beginning to bud, and ended on a broad, curving hummock of bare granite. The boys led me towards a single boulder that sat astride the peak.

By the boulder were several patches of the "nest" the boys had brought into class. And a few feet from that was a shallow indentation that was indeed shaped precisely like the profile of a bird. The lines were quite indistinct and I suspected it might be a fault in the granite formation, but we put a nickel by the bird for scale and took several pictures. The next day the students collaborated on a letter to Memorial describing the area and, along with the picture and sample, sent it to St. John's.

Meanwhile, we decided to put together a collection of rocks from our area. For identification we had to rely on the series of

131

descriptions and hardness tests provided in our books. For the materials, we spent one period scouring the area for the most unusual rocks we could find. The result was hundreds of rocks.

Rocks were piled everywhere in the classroom—in bags, in boxes, on tables, on the floor, on shelves. With the raw material gathered, we began the far more difficult process of identification. We had decided to attach the identified rocks to a huge sheet of plywood after we were done, but the identification process proved more of a task than anyone expected. With much scraping, prying, cracking and discussing, we set about classifying the mounds of rocks we had assembled. At first the kids would approach me regularly.

"I can't figure this one out, Mr. Sawyer. What is it?"

I would take the rock and turn it over in my hands. "Gosh, Louise, I don't know either. Let's go over its characteristics."

"You mean you really don't know?"

"No, I really don't. I told you at the beginning, I didn't know anything about geology."

Since I was obviously no help at all, they finally stopped coming to me and began asking each other. Soon the room resembled a stock exchange as kids held up rocks and yelled for assistance.

"Hey, Max. Does this look like schist?"

"Naw, it's green. I think it's serpentine."

"Anybody know what these gold specks are?"

"Gold?"

I meandered around the room, struggling equally as we tried to decide if this cracked rock was granite or basalt or if that brown thing was sandstone or shale. Leadership came from within the class as a few of the kids became fairly adept at identification. Nonetheless, most of us picked up the basics. Working together, we identified more or less confidently twenty-eight rocks and mounted them proudly on the plywood sheet, which we propped up in the front of the room.

Although our informal approach to geology had produced a substantial, enjoyable learning experience despite (or maybe because of) my lack of knowledge of the subject, I did not dismiss the value of expertise. Fortunately, that appeared as well. While we were working on the rocks, we received a reply to the letter Warrick and Terry had sent concerning our "fossil bird." The letter came from the head of Memorial's geology department, E.R. Neale. Dr. Neale wrote us a long letter which dispelled any fantasies about our "bird" but gave us enough information and encouragement to soften the blow. The specimens from around the bird we had sent, it turned out, were "high rank metamorphic rocks known as schists and gneisses." And the "nest" or "bird tracks" (we hadn't been able to make up our minds which) were "long blade-like crystals of the mineral kyanite" ("Is that anything like kryptonite?" Kevin asked), which had weathered less than the surrounding rock, producing the pattern that had caught our attention.

As for the bird, that was even less spectacular. "The photographs show complex foldings of layers in the gneiss. Sometimes peculiar patterns are produced which superficially resemble plants and animals."

"Superficial!" sniffed Terry. "It sure looks like a bird to me."

Still, Dr. Neale's letter was not entirely negative. "It's nice to hear that you and your students are taking field trips," he wrote. "You are located in a very interesting and complex area of Newfoundland geology—chiefly an area of igneous and metamorphic rocks. The chances of finding fossils there are very remote."

We took solace in the concluding note that a professor Kennedy was coming to the area to do field work for the summer and would drop in on us.

Two weeks later I was called from class and introduced to Dr. Michael Kennedy, head of geology graduate studies at Memorial. He agreed to come into class and have a look at our collection.

The response to Dr. Kennedy was somewhat cool; the students had neither the background nor the interest to follow his sometimes complicated, technical explanations and, I suspected, some of the class was still a little miffed at being told their fossil was only some unusual folds producing a superficial resemblance to a bird. Nonetheless, the class's questions caused him to adjust his presentation to their more basic concerns, and in the end we all got a great deal from this man who had spent ten years doing geological mapping of Newfoundland and was probably as know-ledgeable as anyone in the world on the subject.

"Oh, by the way," Dr. Kennedy said to me later. "I looked at your collection. Not bad."

"Really?" I said, beaming.

"Yeah, you got almost half of them right." But he was serious. He explained to the class that correctly identifying so many rocks was excellent for beginners, and he helped us correct our errors. After his visit to school some of the students began accompanying him on his trips into the country.

Though cold weather and snow flurries still lingered, May was popularly accepted as the official end of winter. Stubborn patches of snow, subfreezing nights, ice floes that blocked the harbour and huge icebergs that loomed on the horizon did not prevent people from deciding it was spring. Activity centred along the waterfront, where boats and lobster pots were readied for the brief lobster season. The slowly warming air broke its winter silence and began to carry the sounds of sputtering outboards, playing children and thumping hammers.

To us, however, May meant that we finally had to decide if we were going to return to Hoberly Cove for another year. Sensing our indecision, the kids began coming over to our apartment more frequently and in greater numbers, bent on convincing us to stay.

"I suppose you'll be leaving next year," Benjamin said sadly one night. "All the good teachers leave. Ever since I was in first grade, every time we'd get a good teacher they'd be gone the next year."

"That's true," Kevin added hastily, noting the look of skepticism on my face. "Why, if you and Mrs. Sawyer leave, everything will go right back to being boring again. Plus we won't have any place to go at night except the cafés," he added, knowing the unsavoury reputation of the small restaurants in town that provided the only places for kids to gather after school.

"Yeah," Warrick said with his mouth full, "and Mrs. Sawyer makes better cake. Besides, it's cheaper to come over here."

It was not an easy decision. Roger was fed up and had resigned

from the high school, taking a newly created and more auto-
nomous position as special education instructor in the elementary school and leaving me without much support. Despite this
development, however, my year had been so positive that I still
favoured staying. Jan, unfortunately, was not nearly so certain.

Teaching had been extraordinarily successful and rewarding for
her. By Easter her kids were so practised in self-direction that
whenever a few finished their assigned work and Jan was with
another group, they would move smoothly onto another project.
And the projects they carried out were phenomenal. Besides
reading their "library" of children's books—a few dozen books
my mother had collected and sent—her students wrote and illustrated their own books, which they bound and placed on the
shelves for other students to read. They also wrote and performed
plays. Entering her class was like stepping into a model classroom; there was a steady hum of energy and activity that was
clearly and unobtrusively organized. In everything that was
going on there was a genuine sense of joy. Jan had extraordinary
rapport with her kids; if she asked a boy or girl a question, the exchange would be friend-to-friend: "Shawn, would you help
Laura with her math?"

"But maid, I'm right in the middle of building a wharf."

The openness and mutual respect in the class had not only produced a relaxed, enjoyable atmosphere but also resulted in reading and math achievement levels never before approached there
in first grade. Half her class had finished all their curriculum
books two thirds of the way through the year. And because she
had carefully avoided placing a negative onus on those who were
progressing at a slower rate, all were accomplished readers by the
end of the year. Her pupils left first grade as enthusiastic and
energetic as when they had entered.

Despite Jan's love for the kids, and their remarkable response
to her, she did not know if she could endure another year of loneliness. "My best friends in this town," she said one night, "are
five years old."

Some of the kids had told us about a house up on the ridge
that was for rent. Since housing was a real factor in our decision

135

(much as we liked the Pikes, we needed a place of our own), we decided to have a look. It was a pink house that sat off by itself in a rolling field just below Morgan's home and garage. As we walked up on the porch at the side of the house, known locally as a "bridge," we looked down on the town spread below us along the loop of coastline. The wind, warming daily, rustled through the new leaves of the aspens surrounding the garden. Far below us we could see tiny white boats cutting noiselessly beyond the rocky fingers of the harbour. The house had a basement and twice the room of our apartment. Benjamin had accompanied us on our trip. "Geez," he mused. "We can have some fun up here. We don't have to worry about noise and there's lots of room."

I was almost sold, especially as the lobster that people brought us and the ever-warming weather tucked memories of the bitter winter farther out of reach. Jan finally agreed that we should stay for another year, but there was still one factor that I wondered about: how much were we wanted? Support had come from the board in Gander, from the kids and to some extent from the parents, but I was reluctant to return to a school where I was going to be at constant odds with the staff and resented by the principal. One night Norman and I were working late, and I took the opportunity to ask him how he felt. "We're, uh, thinking about coming back next year, Norman," I said. He looked up quickly from his papers. "But I really want to know honestly if you would like to see me return or not."

Norman paused thoughtfully, then replied: "I'd be delighted to have you back." He even smiled. "I haven't always agreed with you, but I truthfully think you're good for us. I hope you and Jan decide to come back." With that he put his hand on my shoulder. For some reason I was deeply touched. That evening we determined to stay, sent in our continuing appointment forms and called to take the house. Then Jan went to the bedroom and cried for an hour.

One thing I had vowed to do before we left Hoberly Cove for the summer was to go out with some of the commercial fishermen. In the fall I had gone for an afternoon with Paul Pritchett's father and uncle to haul a few cod traps—the curious net boxes with an open flap that direct the fish into the interior, where they bump around aimlessly until the fishermen haul them into the boat. I had enjoyed the few hours we had spent on the water and had decided that I was ready for a full day of it.

Of the two or three long liners in town, the most prosperous one was owned by Kevin Fillier's father and his two partners. One evening I idly asked Kevin if his dad would mind if I came along with him sometime.

"My God, Sawyer," Kevin exclaimed in alarm. "Why would you want to do a foolish thing like that?" But I persisted, and finally Kevin made the arrangements for me to go out one day around the middle of June. "Are you coming too, Kevin?" I asked.

"Not bloody likely. You won't get me out there tossing around with those smelly, slubby fish sliding all over the deck and the diesel exhaust making you want to puke. Not me, sir."

I should have realized that these fishermen were serious and that I had no business on their boat when Kevin told me his dad left shore at 5:30 in the morning. But I was not to be deterred. I arrived at Kevin's house at 5:15, met his father, Harvey, and accompanied him to a small open boat, where the other two men, John Fillier and Percy Tippett, were already waiting. I shook their hands and climbed aboard and we pushed off.

I remained jaunty for an hour. We went out to their long liner (so named because of its size rather than its fishing method; all the long liners I ever saw used gill nets) and immediately crowded into the tiny cabin below. At 5:45 we moved slowly out of the harbour. I stood at the side of the boat and watched the sun slowly tinge the sky, thinking deeply about the idyllic life of a fisherman. There was no wind to ruffle the calm water, and the men went silently and methodically about their work. Only the thumping of the engine and the wet rustle of the bow cutting through the water disturbed the early morning tranquillity.

That tranquillity, however, lasted only as long as we stayed in the inshore waters, which, unfortunately, we had no intention of doing. Within half an hour the boat began pitching as the sea became more choppy. With ugly memories of our first ferry crossing, I constantly monitored my stomach and was relieved to find everything stable and uncomplaining.

Then the boat stopped. Harvey fished up a red buoy with his hook and pulled the rope over a roller mounted at the end of the boat. The men then hauled the net, which stretched fifty yards to the stern, over the rollers. As the green mesh was pulled from the sea it brought with it the fish that had been snagged in its web. But these fish were not the sleek, flopping creatures we had hauled out of the cod traps; these were dead and stiff, often without eyes, their sickly white flesh torn and decayed. Occasionally large spidery crabs would be pulled up, still feeding on the rotting carcases. Harvey saw me staring at the fish as they were pulled out of the mesh and slid into the hold. "They aren't usually this bad," he told me. "We couldn't get out yesterday because of the weather, so some of these fish have been dead for two days." He shrugged. "Personally, I'll only eat jigged or trapped fish."

The diesel was left idling and now I became aware of the oily exhaust belching out of the short exhaust pipe. The swells that we had cut through easily while moving now had us swinging at anchor and pitched the little boat energetically from side to side.

One hour out of port and I was sick. I threw myself over the tilting edge of the deck and vomited into the water. For the rest of the day I hovered near death. I tried to lie below on the small bunk, but the cramped cabin seemed to only accentuate the rolling of the boat and the noxiousness of the fumes. Above board, I could do little other than hold weakly onto the low railing and hang my head over the side. The men tried to cheer me up. "I was sick once," Percy confided as we headed for the next net, "when I was fifteen. Thought I'd never get back on a boat again, but here I am. You know, there are some fishermen that get sick every time they go out."

During one of my periods on deck, all three men grabbed the net and strained to pull it aboard. Finally a black carcase rolled slowly over the stern and onto the deck. The crabs had already begun to strip the eyes and flesh from the animal, but it was still recognizable as a small dolphin.

"Poor damned thing," Harvey muttered, disentangling it from the net. "We get one of these three or four times a season. I hate like hell to see it."

We were out on the water for fourteen hours. For thirteen of them I was sicker and more miserable than I have been before or since. Incredibly, rather than abating as the day wore on, the nausea and anguish seemed to worsen. Naturally I could not complain; I had asked to come as the men's guest and they had to clean each of their nets.

They finally finished hauling and replacing their last net at 6:30 in the evening, and then turned the boat around for the long trip back. The low bulk of land was the most welcome sight I had ever seen. After an excruciatingly long time, when the land seemed to remain maddeningly distant, we at last pulled up to the community stage, tied up the boat and shut off the engine.

My first impulse was to throw myself off the boat and lie flat on the ground, clutching handfuls of dirt and crying in relief. But either because I felt I owed these men something for putting up with me all day or because I felt a need to redeem myself, I picked up a pitchfork and began helping them unload the boat. By the time we had thrown the last fish into the wheelbarrows that were taken into the shed for weighing, I genuinely felt near collapse.

Kevin had come down to the stage and was not particularly sympathetic. "You want to go out again tomorrow, Mr. Sawyer? I'm sure Dad would be glad to have you. They'll be leaving at 5:30."

I still had the pitchfork in my hand but felt too weak to heave it. I thanked the three fishermen as sincerely as I could and then pulled myself feebly onto the stage. For the first time in fourteen hours, what I was standing on was not moving. My knees buckled and I fell. I picked myself up shakily and with Kevin's help tottered down the road. I eased myself into the car and drove slowly up to the house.

When I woke up the next day I still felt weak and shaky. As I tremblingly sat at the table trying to force coffee down my throat I realized that Harvey and his partners had been at it again for four hours by the time I had even struggled out of bed. For four

139

months they kept up this schedule, fifteen hours a day, six days a week. I dismissed fishing as a possible future vocation.

Once we had made our decision to stay, the rest of the school year seemed determined to convince us that we had been fools to pass up a chance to get out. Most of the trouble grew out of disagreements over in-school final exams, which were slated to last an entire week. It was not a new argument; from the beginning, I had questioned the necessity of mandatory finals in every class. My point was that a course which revolves around an individual rather than a standardized program is far more difficult to "test" than a traditional course. I had not been simply arguing the principle of the matter, either. The proposed single final exam was to account for fifty per cent of a student's mark; it was a kind of pistol at the head of students that I felt would hinder the trust and openness I desired. Furthermore, it would force me to fall back on a measurement tool I was trying to avoid—the comparison and ranking of students on the basis of their performance on a standardized test. Also, it seemed impossible to contain in a written exam the learning objectives I had established. As writing and thinking experiences, my Deep Thought quizzes made sense, but should one of these be half a student's entire mark for the year? Finally, knowing now the way the kids tended to panic on tests, I was afraid for them. I feared that they would close up again and withdraw, handing in blank sheets that would not even allow me room for juggling.

My arguments went largely ignored. Since Roger was faced with the grade eleven province-wide public exams, he was not as personally involved in the issue of in-school finals and did not participate in the debate. In the end the rest of the teachers supported the traditional formula. I had to give the exams. But the least I could do was to try to make the rest of the staff think about the implications of the exam system. "If we're going to evaluate one-half of a student's entire growth for a year on the basis of one two-hour session," I said, "I think it is only fair that we give them the opportunity to do the same for us."

"What!" Norman and Calvin were startled. "That's ridiculous. What basis do they have for evaluating us?"

"I suggest they have at least as much basis for evaluating our performance as teachers as we do for determining theirs as students."

"No bloody student will ever judge me," Calvin exploded.

"You seem to have forgotten something, Don," Norman said. "As adults and teachers we're different from students. It is our profession and our responsibility to offer guidance and to provide some way of charting progress."

"Certainly we have to provide feedback for kids so that they can see their behaviour more clearly and adjust it to meet their own needs. To me that's guidance, but that should be an on-going process, not something we hammer them with at the end of the year. And for many of them the feedback they receive will be massively negative—flunking a course or even being told they have matured and grown so little that they must repeat the entire year. All that will accomplish is frustration and lowered self-esteem."

Calvin had had enough. "You're always talking about success and never flunking kids, about damaging their delicate egos," he snarled. "But I'm telling you now that's crap. The world isn't a place where everyone co-operates and loves each other. It's a competitive, hard world. You either learn how to succeed or you fail. And not failing these kids in school is a lie. You're not preparing them for life by passing them all in school, because life isn't like that." He sat back and glowered at me.

"You're right, Calvin. Like it or not we are living in a competitive society, I agree." I paused and sighed. It seemed as if we had been through this a dozen times. "But ask yourself one question: How do people learn to compete effectively in a competitive society, by experiencing success or failure? Does a person who comes out of school feeling that he is capable and successful, or a person who leaves feeling he is a failure and incompetent, stand a better chance of making it in society?"

Calvin shoved his seat back, picked up his books and stomped out of the room. The meeting broke up. The finals were still mandatory for all subjects, but I decided to follow through with the idea of a form that would enable my students to evaluate me.

141

At least the results of that evaluation provided me with some much needed reinforcement. The responses to the twenty-two questions I gave to my classes were overwhelmingly positive. They indicated that the students felt better about themselves and good about the year we had spent together. With my tens I took the process one step further. I wanted to give them a personal evaluation of how I felt the class had developed, and provide them with a chance to respond to my remarks. I wrote up my feelings on a stencil, listing my observations under two headings, "positive things" ("People seem more willing to think things out for themselves and express their ideas; People are more willing to try something new—there's not as much fear of failure") and "disappointments" ("Not the consideration and understanding for each other there should be; I've had to resort to more of an authoritarian 'teacher' role than I'd hoped," etc.), and the students wrote their responses on the back. The results were a fairly frank appraisal of my growth and the growth of the students, from their point of view. Overall, too, there seemed to be a greater feeling of honesty—we had thrust our feelings about each other, good and bad, into the open. We regarded each other with a new sense of respect and candour.

The finals were far more difficult for me to produce. I spent many hours preparing papers which I hoped accurately reflected the way the classes had unfolded. My exams asked for a discussion of education, a description of the noises around them as they wrote; critiques of films they had viewed and books they had read; analyses of advertisements and the way they used language to persuade; a question on how the student would attack Newfoundland's socio-economic problems; a character sketch of the people in photographs stapled onto the papers; questions on rocks, Beothuck Indians, class projects, social roles, environment, the landscape of Mars; words to define, and dozens of optional essay topics. When I finally put them together, despite the alternatives I had provided on many questions, I was terrified that the five- or six-page tests, with enclosed ads and pictures, would so intimidate the kids that I would end up with nothing to work with.

I spent several days trying to prepare my classes by urging them to relax and assuring them that they would have little trouble. "Just write," I pleaded. But I was totally unprepared for the climate of the exams. One hundred and fifty desks were lined up in five rows in the gym. Students were marched in at 9:00 and 12:00, ordered to be quiet, handed their tests, and watched closely by the teacher-monitors, who were supposed to slip quietly between the rows to frustrate cheating. One student wrote on his paper that he was "trapped in a world of think... I feel like a charred cinder floating in space." I was glad now that I had decided to flippantly name my test "Return of Deep Thought Quiz" and scatter dumb jokes throughout the paper.

In the end, my anxiety proved unfounded. One girl wrote: "Paper too long. Don't take it as a slap, but you gave us all think questions, which I agree with, but a few too many." Almost every question was tried by every student nonetheless, and the responses were generally well thought out, organized and expressed. The fact that they had successfully handled the complicated questions, despite the suffocating atmosphere of the exams, proved to me just how far we had come since the first of the year.

Even our final staff meeting went fairly smoothly. Most of the staff had already concluded from their own experience that, in most cases, keeping a student back to repeat an entire year did far more harm than good, but flunking and repeating three or four classes was still a very real possibility in many students' cases. I proudly revealed that I was able to pass every student in my classes.

The response to this news was milder than it had been earlier in the year; we were all getting tired, I concluded. There was still a flurry of criticism when I announced my grades. But I was not budging.

"Look. Every kid in grade ten could write the names of five books he had read this year, and compose a critique. At the beginning of the year most of them hadn't read five books in their lives. They analyzed advertisements with insight and understanding. They knew difficult vocabulary, demonstrated reading skills, wrote imaginatively, and showed an improved understanding of their society, themselves and their world. Every kid here showed me that he met my criteria for success. They satisfied and exceeded my expectations."

Still, some of my kids were flunked in many subjects not taught by me. They would go on, but some had to repeat specific classes. I knew that many of these would not be back.

But the relief of the school year ending overrode whatever disappointment I felt about the final outcome. Jan was exhausted. Though first and second grades had been spared from finals, third grade and up were put through the same procedure as we had gone through in the high school. Jan was tired of arguing and worrying about it all. We both just wanted to roll our new tent into the back seat of the SAAB, pack a few clothes, and start unwinding our way west.

A few days after school was out, we left for the summer. Carl and May stood in their door and waved as we passed through the garden, and Enos Pike looked up from his potatoes and shouted goodbye. Three boys with fishing poles walking along the road grinned and waved frantically as we headed up the hill. Everywhere clusters of kids waved at us from the side of the road. Ralph Whiteway, one of Jan's first graders, stood on top of a rock in front of his house and shouted "Goodbye, Mrs. Sawyer." I rounded the hill and turned onto the high road by Morgan's. Morgan had seen us coming and stood by the road.

"Take care of yourself, now," he said as we stopped. "Come on back so I can come down there and drink some of your beer for a change." Morgan's youngest boy appeared by his father's leg. "See you this fall, Mrs. Sawyer."

9

"Tomorrow is school and I am sick to the heart thinking about it"

By the end of the summer we were eager to get to Hoberly Cove, so we paused only briefly in Gander to pick up a few supplies, then immediately made our way out the Port Warford road. Rain had succeeded in further eroding the road, transforming sections into an open ditch. Other parts were rutted, with jarring ridges like a gigantic ripple-cut potato chip. When the wheels plunged into potholes, sheets of muddy water flew into the air, covering the windshield and trickling through cracks around the windows.

By the time we pulled into Hoberly Cove and parked the SAAB outside our new house, we were worn out, wet, and still tingling from the constant jolting. The sun had already set, so we stumbled wearily up the back stairs in the dark, unlocked the door and slumped, tired and dejected, onto the old brown sofa that was pushed up against one plain wall in the bare living room.

We had just sunk into the cushions when I heard footsteps thunder up the stairs outside, then a loud knock. I opened the door to find the bridge crowded with faces I could only dimly make out in the dark.

"Hi, Mr. Sawyer," called Terry Rowe, one of my last year's grade eight students, "We heard you were back in town."

"How could you have heard that? We've only been here five minutes."

"We've got real good ears," Kevin offered.

"And we've been listening real hard," laughed Warrick.

"Can we bring your stuff in from the car?" asked Ben Collins.

"Well, sure, if you don't mind." In minutes the four of them had cleaned out the SAAB and moved everything into the middle of the living room. As they hustled in and out of the house, filling us in on the doings of the summer, the atmosphere brightened.

After prowling through the house like prospective buyers, the boys finally seemed satisfied that the place was liveable, and prepared to leave.

"I'm glad you're back, Sawyer," Warrick said as he left. "Things were getting boring around here."

"I think," Jan said to me, "that we've been welcomed back."

Morgan woke us up in the morning. "Get up, Sawyers," he yelled as he stomped through the kitchen. "It's a lovely bright day outside and there's no time for lying in bed."

I poked my head warily out of the bedroom to see Morgan sitting at the kitchen table drinking a beer. "Morgan, how the hell can you drink beer at this time of the morning?"

"My son," he said with mock solemnity. "A man has only so many chances to drink beer in this life, and if he misses one it's gone forever. What's more, I brought you one."

I groaned and limped off towards the bathroom. Soon we were drinking beer in our living room in the bright sun that poured through the enormous picture window facing Morgan's house and the high road. "This is a wonderful house, Don boy," Morgan enthused. "And look how close you are to the garage. Why, I can even make house calls."

The house really was fine. It had three bedrooms, one of which we had decided to convert into a study, a large kitchen and living room, a long hall just about right for a dart board, a partially completed basement with the beginnings of a shop, and a front door that opened into thin air.

146

"Morgan, why does everyone's front door open to nothing? Almost every house in this town has a front door with no stairs or bridge attached. If anyone walked out of them he'd break his neck!"

Morgan looked at me seriously. "That's the idea. You see we call them mother-in-law doors. If your mother-in-law comes and overstays her welcome, you ask her to leave by the front door. She gets the hint."

I looked at him closely. "Is that the truth, Morgan?"

He laughed noiselessly until his eyes closed into two neat crescents. "Absolutely."

The semi-wild horse herd that trotted unrestricted about town chose the second morning to pay us a mass visit. We had unpacked and cleaned the house the first day and piled all the trash into six large plastic bags, which we left outside for the garbage truck. The next morning I was working in the living room when I heard something rubbing against the window, which was five or six feet above the ground. Puzzled, I pulled the drapes open and stared directly into the startled eyes of a large brown horse. He snorted in irritation and strolled back across the yard, picking his way between the twenty or so others lying on the grass. The six garbage bags had been ripped open and their contents strewn all over the yard.

Between Morgan and the steady flow of kids through the house, Jan and I had little time to be lonesome in the last few days before school began. Our reintroduction to school was less pleasant. I found that Norman's tentative timetable had relieved me of all history and geography, and included physical education for the entire school. I was also given three periods a week for remedial reading, though I had no idea what that should entail, and English 9 and 10. One block had been left blank.

A little miffed at losing my social studies (I had heard rumours that some teachers were concerned my history students were ill prepared since they had not received a good foundation in ancient Mesopotamian or medieval German history in my class), I asked Norman about the open time. "What's going on?" I asked suspiciously. "What's this open block all about?"

"I'd like you to take English 11 this year, Don."

I squirmed uneasily. "You know how I feel about public exams, Norman. I'd really rather not."

"You're the only real English teacher we have," Norman said. "Like it or not, you have the best chance of getting them through the exams."

Public exams had come to disturb me deeply. Only people who saw learning as the tightly regulated acquisition of packaged information and skills, I felt, could still view province-wide tests as legitimate. I thought grimly of their effects in Newfoundland. The public exams had served admirably to maintain the privileged status of a small economic and social elite while presenting the appearance of a fair and unassailable meritocracy.

"There's one more thing," Norman continued as I fumed to myself about the inequities of these exams. "It looks like we may be able to determine fifty per cent of the final marks this year. That's not certain, though."

I brightened, but only slightly. In the past, a student's entire mark, his very graduation, was determined entirely by four or five standardized two-hour exams at the end of the year. Even with the possible change, the pressures would remain largely the same. But more intolerable was the thought of my former grade ten students labouring under Norman in English. With Roger gone, I had become the English department. I sighed heavily. "I guess I don't have much choice."

Besides teaching, I also became intramural sports co-ordinator, official librarian, and secretary of our athletic league, and I found that I had been named by Russell Taylor to something called the Integrated Studies Special Interest Committee. There had been science, geography and English special interest committees before, but this was a new one. I had no idea what it was about, nor did the rest of the staff.

If I was somewhat distressed by my class assignments, Jan was crushed. Whereas the year before there had been two first-grade classes, this year the board was trying to get away with one. So Jan ended up with thirty-eight first graders and was moved out with Emma Pritchett, the kindergarten teacher, to the old clapboard two-room school behind the United Church hall. Though the switch later proved a blessing, at the time it simply served to reinforce her feelings of isolation. And having thirty-eight first graders was obviously too much. For the first week she dissolved into tears of frustration and weariness each night. Only the eventual transfer of five students to the second grade, a move Jan resisted until it became clear there was no alternative, saved her from total collapse. And she began almost at once to bring parents into the classroom as volunteers. As she slowly regained her confidence, she saw the possibilities her new independence offered. She and Emma Pritchett became a team unto themselves, and some of the community's most exciting educational happenings occurred in the little clapboard school stranded behind the deserted United Church hall in the marsh.

Before we could begin the school year, we had to endure one last ordeal. As promised the year before, I.Q. tests were to be given to all students in Hoberly Cove. Jan threatened to refuse rather than subject her kids, at the age of six, to the tension and anxiety that inevitably accompanies the administration of such "measurements." I protested bitterly, not only that the tests were culturally biased and totally inappropriate in the Newfoundland context but also that the idea of measuring people's intelligence was absurd in the first place.

"Did you know that the first tests had to be adjusted because they kept showing that women were on an average ten points dumber than men?"

"Well, there you go," laughed Leo Fillier, a new staff member originally from Hoberly Cove, who had graduated from Memorial the year before.

"The point is," I continued, "that all these things measure is people's educational background and how closely the subject's exposure and environment correlate with the values and skills demanded by the test. It doesn't have anything to do with intellectual potential. Did you know these things were first designed for use in screening soldiers for the French Army?"

Leo looked at me dubiously. "No, but so what?"

"They were primarily designed to single out conformists: those most capable of unquestioningly following orders. Look at them—there's no value placed on imagination, creative problem solving or sensitivity."

"I don't know about that," Willis said. "In the past, the scores have lined up almost exactly with grades."

"Sure, school success requires the same sort of characteristics and skills—conformity, mastery of material, reading skills, middle-class values. Also there's such a thing as self-fulfilling prophecy. If you test a kid in first grade and he scores low, there's a tendency for teachers and parents to expect that kid to perform poorly. Everything in his environment thenceforward subtly conspires to convince him that he's dumb, just as the test indicated. That tendency is continued and magnified throughout his school career. He finds he's in the slow reading group, the teacher smiles at him less, his grades are low, he flunks grades. What else do you expect? No wonder there's a high correlation.

"And that's the real tragedy. Because even if they did actually reflect some sort of intellectual differentiation, so what? Would low scores justify turning kids off learning? To discourage them? To steer them into vocational tracks? What do we know once we have these tests? How does it better help us to meet each student's needs?"

I had expected no answers, and I got none. All I got was a stack of tests.

The results were predictable. The school as a whole ranked in the "dull normal" range, and only a few managed to penetrate into the above-average category. "Look at this," Willis mumbled, as he and several other staff members pored intently over the print-outs. "Gordie Burt has the highest I.Q. in the school." Gordie being Norman's son, his score did not seem curious to me at all.

I finally had a chance to confront the new school board special education co-ordinator, who turned out to be a very reasonable and likeable man, about the results.

"I've worked with these kids," I said. "These are some of the brightest, most alive, creative kids I've ever seen. Yet they scored consistently below average on these damned I.Q. tests. How can you claim they're legitimate?"

"I don't," he replied simply, "because they obviously aren't. Newfoundland generally scores eight points below the national average, while the outport scores are even lower. Obviously they're biased toward urban middle-class kids. You ought to see the results when these are given to Indian children."

I was flabbergasted. "Well, why are you giving them then?"

"Because we need the money. We're allowed so much special education money for every child showing an I.Q. below the "dull normal" range. It's just that simple."

I was somewhat mollified until Norman came up to me. "You know, Don," he said, "you're always talking about how smart these kids are. I hope these tests have shown you what we're really up against."

And the situation in the elementary school had been even worse. Jan had finally agreed to administer the tests after a great deal of pressure from Hector, the principal. That night she had come home thoroughly upset.

Before she had passed the exams out she had tried to depressurize the whole process by down playing the test's importance and making it into a game. Just about the time she had reduced the apprehension in the room, Hector had thundered in.

"These tests are very important," he warned sternly. "You must be very quiet and not look on anyone else's paper or Mrs. Sawyer will rip it up. You must try very hard to get the answers right." Jan said she could see the terror mount on the faces of the kids as he spoke.

Apparently suspicious of Jan, Hector remained in the room while she passed out the exams, further heightening the pressure. She began the test, much of which involved the oral reading of words which the kids were supposed to match with pictures on their test. But when a little boy she had been watching, who had grown more confused and tense as the grueling session went on, finally dropped his head onto his arms and had begun crying, she couldn't take any more. She handed the book to Hector, went to the boy and comforted him, telling him the test was silly and unimportant. When he finally calmed down, she had walked from the room and cried herself.

151

"And the things they were expected to know!" she railed angrily. "It was ridiculous. They had a picture of four people and the word was gypsy. None of the kids have ever even heard of a gypsy, much less have any idea what one looks like. Another one was trombone. They were supposed to pick out a trombone from a trumpet, a clarinet and a tuba. The only instruments most of these kids have ever seen are tambourines and harmonicas."

But that is how it was decided who was bright and who was dull in the first grade. And the children's scores were duly inscribed in their records and on their psyches. The elementary scores were even lower than the high school's; the selection process had already removed some of the "dull normals" by the time they hit the halls of higher learning. Jan's class, it turned out, was made up largely of "trainable and educable retardeds."

"Do you know what Cecil said at the staff meeting after the scores came back?" Jan asked. "He said it just goes to show that these kids need more discipline and more of the basics. He said, 'We can't afford any of this modern education nonsense when we have children this dull. These children need training.' I was so angry I had to walk out of the room."

One of the first things I did in September was to reorganize the library. I spent a Saturday with eight volunteers unpacking, stamping, and classifying the new books that had arrived. We now had nearly two thousand books on the shelves and were able to remove the last of the old volumes we had left as fillers. As we packed them away forever, I marvelled again at the bizarre collection of books that had somehow found their way onto these shelves.

Besides books, we also began ordering magazines with money raised and donated. Fifty dollars was given by my mother and her friends in Detroit—who, I am sure, saw Jan and me as missionaries working in some exotic native village. In all, twenty-two subscriptions began slipping quietly into Hoberly Cove.

As for English 11 and the public exams, I eventually decided that I had to be honest about my reservations and fears by putting my feelings forward to the class right from the start. I also needed to know what the students' priorities were and what they wanted of me, so I prepared a short statement for the first day of class. Essentially I told them what they already knew—that the year before had been loose and in my opinion successful, bound only by our imagination and initiative, and that despite the threat of public exams I would like to continue the philosophies and objectives of the previous year. I also noted my two primary objectives: providing a relaxed but challenging atmosphere conducive to the experience of education, and getting each one of them through the exams. Then I asked them to write down their criticisms, priorities and concerns, how they wanted the class structured, and what changes they thought were necessary.

To my surprise, their responses reflected far less apprehension towards the exams than I had anticipated. None of them advocated a slavish adherence to the curriculum for the entire year, though most were obviously concerned. "I don't like to say it," one girl wrote, "but I guess it's back to the same old stuff this year. I liked what we did last year but it isn't what we need for passing."

"First of all," I said to the class, "I want to dispel what I think are some false notions. What we did last year was not wasted. Didn't you learn a great deal about how to attack problems and solve them effectively? You learned how to size up a situation and adapt to it. You learned how to work independently, and many of you rediscovered that you can think. I'm telling you, with those skills most of you could handle any reasonable test tossed your way."

Everyone beamed happily. "Unfortunately these aren't going to be reasonable exams." Sudden consternation. "But you can learn what you need to know to pass that exam in two months, one month, even a few weeks." Now there was only scornful disbelief. "I'm serious. We'll read the necessary material off and on throughout the year, but the biggest part will be learning how to take the test. Remember, they're not interested in what you write on these things, just how you put it down. So, what we'll do towards the end is concentrate on mastering the form. Meanwhile, relax, enjoy yourselves and maybe we'll really learn something."

The beginnings of remedial reading were less auspicious. The year before I had complained constantly that reading was a critical area in the school, and one that deserved more attention, especially for those with serious problems. Much to my chagrin, I now found myself in charge of a token remedial reading program. Because nothing like it had been tried before, there were no materials at all in the school. In addition, I had had no experience whatsoever in developmental reading. Still, because there was such a clear need for something, I resolved to do what I could.

Whereas I knew very little about teaching reading, I did have preconceptions I had picked up from my own schooling. First and foremost, I had learned to view reading instruction as a mechanical process that had to be taught to reluctant learners through constant drill under duress. For some reason, when it came to remedial reading, I was unable to generalize from Jan's experience or even my own teaching experiences. Remedial reading was not fun. As I had heard elsewhere, even bribes would probably be required to persuade students to participate. It took one session with Winston Fillier to show me that teaching remedial reading was like anything else: in the end I was teaching people, and how I dealt with them was more critical than the content.

I had ordered some material I hoped would prove interesting and readable while focussing on the primary reading difficulties the students were experiencing. In the meantime I was calling in students I suspected had serious reading problems. I started with my grade nines, since I knew them best, asking them to read passages from our English books. If they encountered a great deal of difficulty, I moved them down through graded material, thus gaining a rough idea of where they were in reading skills.

When I called Winston in and asked him to read he sat silently across from me and stared at the book. No amount of coaxing seemed to budge him. Well prepared for this eventuality, I pulled a quarter from my pocket and thrust it across the table.

"If you'll read for me, Winston," I said condescendingly, "I'll give you a quarter."

Winston looked at me with distaste. He slid the quarter back across the table. "Mr. Sawyer, there's a reason I don't like to read aloud. I'm not very good at it and it embarrasses me. I won't read for a quarter. I'll read because I want to." His eyes flashed with anger and pride, then lowered to the open book on the table. He began to painfully fight through the words before him. I took my quarter and put it back into my pocket.

"Winston," I said, "I'm really ashamed of myself. I'm sorry." He stopped reading, looked at me briefly and turned back to the book.

It was the first and last time I attempted overt behavioural modification.

In the end, I found that nearly two thirds of my grade nine students were unable to read and understand the curriculum material with ease. I saw that I would have to supplement and select the assigned reading in my English class, and that the need for remedial reading was not restricted to a very few. Obviously a broad range of reading levels existed within the one class, while the material was geared to a single level. The only homogeneity was in the minds of the curriculum planners.

At first I tried to continue pulling those with the most serious problems out of class in groups of five and six. I noticed, however, that the attitude of those students I pulled out became negative and many of them turned sullen and unco-operative, a disturbing situation since they had been alive and responsive until I began the reading group. I finally asked them how they felt about being removed from their class.

They glanced quickly at each other through lowered eyes. No one spoke for a while. "I don't like it," Sterling blurted suddenly. "It makes me feel small and dumb. I hate it."

"When a teacher calls my name for me to go to reading class," Clara Pritchett said quietly, "I just want to disappear into the floor."

The anger and pain poured out of them. "It's just like in fourth grade when we were put in a special group and made to use grade three books," one boy said. "We were put off in a corner and I felt really bad."

I dissolved the group and took the problem to the entire class.

Warrick listened intently, then spoke. "I think we should all go into reading groups. I mean, we can all improve our reading, can't we?"

"Yeah," Eunice Fillier offered, "we all know that some people read better than others. It's just when we're made to feel bad about it that it really matters. We're all doing the best we can."

We took a vote and the class unanimously decided to rotate into reading sessions. I divided them up randomly into groups, and during my reading periods each group met me in the library. Other teachers had no need to call names aloud; the students knew when they were assigned, and it was only on rare occasions that someone failed to attend.

In the reading classes the attention was individualized. Since the students were more relaxed and less defensive, I was now able to work effectively with those kids who had serious problems. Some students read novels or helped others who were having more trouble. Sometimes we worked as a group on general skills, such as comprehension and context clues. The reading class became a way of teaching reading in a humane atmosphere. It ended up pulling the kids together, reinforcing co-operation and acceptance, rather than further alienating and dividing them. Again, I felt I had learned more than anyone.

While I worked things out with my classes, the staff room was seized by another struggle. Premier Joey Smallwood, who had led Newfoundland into confederation with Canada in 1949, had called an election for the end of October. Joey had parlayed his role as foremost advocate of Confederation into a twenty-two-year stranglehold for his Liberal party on the provincial government; at one point the opposition was reduced to a total of three seats. But now it was different; in this election it was believed that Joey could be beaten, and the community and province were gripped with political excitement.

Our district had remained one of the staunchest Liberal ridings on the island throughout the years since Confederation, never failing to return Liberal candidates to St. John's by staggering margins. "You could run Mickey Mouse in Fogo District and he'd win by a landslide if he was a Liberal," Norman had once re-marked.

Even long-time Liberals like Norman were looking to the Progressive Conservatives, and John Lundrigan, our well-liked Conservative M.P., was in the district trying to drum up support for the rather unspectacular P.C. candidate—a United Church minister who claimed he had heard the call to come to Newfoundland while crossing the Lion's Gate bridge in B.C. "You see, Don," Norman explained, "Joey hates fishing and fishermen. His government hasn't spent enough on the fishing industry to worry about. When he was elected he came on the radio and said, 'Burn your boats, boys, you'll never have to go fishing again.' And ever since then he's squandered millions of dollars trying to make Newfoundland into an industrial centre, while allowing fishing to die.

"Newfoundland is a Liberal province," he concluded, "but it's time to get Joey out once and for all."

Joey had other ideas. In October he announced that he would hold a major rally in Hoberly Cove in the high school gym, and the excitement rippled through the town like a mounting storm. To my disappointment, I discovered that a volleyball tournament in Twillingate had been scheduled the same day that Joey would be in town, and no amount of pleading could get it switched. I resigned myself to missing a major performance by "the only living Father of Confederation." Joey reportedly hit his oratorical stride only when speaking in front of outport audiences, long his power base. Though we did well in the tournament and enjoyed the rugged beauty of New World Island, all afternoon and evening I thought about Joey flying into Hoberly Cove in his private helicopter.

The next morning Roger called me early. "Did you hear what happened last night?" he asked excitedly.

"No. Was it interesting?"

"Was it interesting! I've never seen anything like it in my life."

"Well?" I said impatiently, "what happened?"

"First of all the place was jammed. People had come from Warrendale, Heston, Northport, Long Arm, all over the area. People were standing—packed against the walls. Even the aisles were full of kids sitting on the floor. There must have been a thousand people in that gym."

"A thousand?" Once we had had a crowd of two hundred for a volleyball game, and that seemed uncomfortably crowded.

"And then Joey got started. I recorded it, and I'm glad I did, because no one would believe it otherwise. He started slow, reviewing everything he'd done for the people of Newfoundland, taking personal credit for unemployment insurance, family allowance and welfare, then built to a climax. When he had everyone worked into a frenzy he began talking about God, implying that he'd been personally appointed by God to oversee the destiny of Newfoundland, and that he was in constant, personal touch with the Lord himself.

"At this point women were moaning and people were shouting and the whole place was in an uproar. Suddenly a few middle-aged women ran for the stage and tried to kiss his feet!"

"Come on, Roger," I said in frank disbelief. "You know you're exaggerating."

"I am not. People tried to drag the women away, but Joey said, 'Let them be. Let them touch me,' and he extended his hand like the pope for these women to kiss."

The election itself turned out to be as extraordinary as Joey's visit. Despite Morgan's prediction that Joey would never be turned out of office, the results seemed to show that the Liberals had finally been ousted. Although they easily retained their seats in our riding, they did not fare as well in other parts of the province.

Of forty-two seats, the Liberals won twenty while the Conservatives took twenty-one (a single seat had been picked up by the newly formed New Labrador Party). But appearances in Newfoundland politics, we learned, can be deceiving. Insisting that the election was still in doubt, Joey simply refused to relinquish power, sending the Conservatives into fits of frustration. A tangle of re-counts and shifting alliances ended up being debated in the courts and garages of the province for two months. And though we shared the momentary excitement and brief turmoil, the outcome was largely meaningless to the people of

158

Hoberly Cove. Life in the outports, as always, would remain largely unaffected by the politics in St. John's. Despite often heard claims that Newfoundlanders are the most politicized people in the world, only an event such as Joey's visit had any direct impact, and that, as Roger indicated, was more of a religious than a political experience.

My cousin George had come up to visit from Alabama during this period, in a station wagon loaded with photographic gear. George visited my grade ten English class, since we were reading *To Kill a Mockingbird*, and spoke on racism in the south. This was a concept that most of the kids had a difficult time grasping until one girl related the snubs she had encountered as a Newfoundlander while living in Toronto. "My dad couldn't take it any more," she finished, "and we had to come back." The discrimination she had experienced was not as deep and brutal as racism, perhaps, but the idea was the same.

The reality of the remoteness, self-containment and insularity of Hoberly Cove was always brought home to me most sharply by the kids. One day in English we were discussing a story about a boy who finally overcame his fears and climbed a water tower. I had thoroughly enjoyed the story and could not understand everyone's indifference to this boy's struggles to prove his courage to himself. But no matter what I tried, I received no response. Finally I asked one boy if he would be scared climbing a water tower. "I don't know," he answered sheepishly. "I don't know what one is." Neither did anyone else. There were no illustrations for the story and there were no water towers in the area. Only one boy had ever seen one—while living in Toronto.

The implications of a similar incident involving some of Roger's special education students were almost shocking. Roger, along with a very capable woman from St. John's named Celia Wilson, had begun a special program for kids who were "not benefitting from the regular school program." ("If we followed those guidelines," Roger confided, "the whole damned school would qualify.") The fourteen students in the program ranged in age from seven to fifteen, and while two of them were probably suffering from retardation or other physiological problems, the great majority were victims only of emotional problems and learning blocks. Many of the problems grew from narrow, unsupportive home and school environments. To expose the kids to the world outside Hoberly Cove—none of the students had ever been more than a few miles away—Roger and Celia planned a day trip into Gander. They were only able to get permission for ten of their students, but with them in their cars they set out to tour the city and airport of Gander.

Since the trip seemed innocuous in the extreme, the results were hard to believe. One girl, who was about ten, began to cry when they got to the paved section of the road. "She'd never seen pavement before, and it scared her," Roger explained. "She thought it was a natural phenomenon." Another girl, about twelve, was so frightened at seeing an airplane land that she screamed, closed her eyes and clapped her hands over her ears to shut out the noise. One child became so excited by the people in Gander—a town of about eight thousand—that she vomited in the car. In a restaurant, several became too flustered to order.

One of the effects of Hoberly Cove's isolation was a high degree of fatalism. A somewhat fatalistic attitude was understandable and maybe even necessary in traditional Newfoundland, but with the twentieth century crashing into even the remotest outports, it now simply rendered the people vulnerable and passive. This fatalism was evident in students' feelings about their inability to change the community, the school, or even their own lives. Whereas a few were able to somehow develop the clarity and sense of personal worth that allowed them to no longer view the larger society as terrifying and incomprehensible, for many the future held only fear and uncertainty.

Even the religions in the community tended to support the view of life as being frightening and incontrovertible. One boy, a Pentecostal who always seemed somehow haunted, responded to a question about what the future held and what he felt he needed to cope with that future by writing: "There is no use thinking about the future because the world is going to end very soon. There is no reason to solve the world's problems because it is doomed anyway." A frightening view of the world by a frightened sixteen-year-old boy.

Not all the kids were like this, of course. On Guy Fawkes' night we heard a knock on our door. When I opened it there was no one on the bridge, but in the field right by our house I could see the dim outline of a man, apparently with his hair on fire. Suddenly his head erupted in a flash of fire and sparks, and I nearly fainted. While I gripped the door handle in fright, Warrick and Kevin came out from under the porch, laughing. They had built a frame, stuffed a suit of old clothes with straw, and filled the bag that served as the scarecrow's head with gunpowder. Then they had ignited the shredded paper that was glued to the bag, knocked on our door, and waited. The effect, I am sure, was what they had expected.

On a typical evening shortly after Roger and his students had returned from Gander, Kevin was drawing at my desk while Warrick poked through our bookshelf. Terry was playing his guitar quietly in the living room and Maxwell was heard hammering on something in the basement. Ben leafed through *Psychology Today* and *Spiderman*. Jan was baking cookies in the kitchen.

Kevin brought his drawings to me for approval—one showed a caricature of a leering Trudeau with the caption "Blood, sweat and girls I always say"—then began fooling with the tape recorder, taping Terry's singing. I accompanied Terry on his next song by pounding somewhat rhythmically on a trunk. Kevin picked up a plastic flute and began playing along. Attracted by the noise, Jan came in and began playing another flute while Ben and Warrick started blowing on kazoos. Maxwell grabbed some wind chimes and joined in, and we began one of the strangest jam sessions every recorded.

We sang, howled, laughed, chanted and hummed for an hour, and the resulting music, captured on tape, was astonishingly catchy. We dubbed the work "Transcendental Fish and Brewis Boogie Blues," decided to call ourselves "The Newfie Kazoo and Drum Ensemble," and began to make plans for cutting our first record. When I played the tape in class a few days later, though, most of the kids were certain it was the product of African natives.

Around 9:30 Warrick's mother phoned for him, so Warrick stuffed a few extra cookies into his pockets and started down the hill. The rest were reluctant to leave, still clinging to the after-glow of the evening, but slowly they drifted out the door, shouting good night as they disappeared into the dark. Ben was the last to leave. "Thanks for the cookies, Mr. and Mrs. Sawyer. And thanks for the evening. I sure had a good time."

I didn't understand exactly what we were providing or what our role had become, but I knew it had spilled far beyond the confines of the school.

As I walked back into the living room, I found a letter that Warrick had written. On the bottom of the paper he had drawn a picture of the school "being burnt and blown into peaces"; flames and smoke were boiling out the windows while more rockets rained on the roof. "Dear Sawyer," he had written. "Here I am sitting down watching some bloody fool celebrating his birthday on TV. You have jut come and sat down beside me, and boy do you looked pooped. Your wife is over writing something. Everything is still. My mother just called me as usual. I enjoyed your wife's cookies very well. Tomorrow is school and I am sick to the heart thinking about it."

10

"You're born into it and it into you"

"What we need is to develop more discipline. And the military has shown us that the only way to do that is through drill and obedience to command." I listened in disbelief. This was not a meeting of canine obedience school instructors but the term's first conference of physical education teachers in our district. My hope had been that this speaker, an East Indian, might have escaped the jock syndrome I had observed in most of the teachers who had already spoken. But as he continued, my heart sank: "I have my students snap to attention as soon as I blow my whistle. Then a monitor I have chosen inspects each student to make sure his uniform is proper. That way there is no wasted time, and I never have any problems."

"Yes, but are you trying to produce well-adjusted young people or soldiers?" Everyone turned toward the questioner, the only woman present—who naturally had been appointed recording secretary. "I, too, have no problems," she continued in her soft voice, "yet I try to treat my students with respect. Surely we have time in our classes to be kind."

There was an awkward silence, finally broken when another man remarked, "You have to remember Mrs., uh, Milord (we all wore gummed name tags that said "Hi! My name is _____"), "that girls are different. They don't require as much control as boys, especially in high school."

She looked at the man and said, "I do teach high school boys."

For the rest of the morning we debated the essential question that had been raised: were we to be more concerned with control and discipline or the physical and concomitant emotional development of our students? There seemed to be little chance of reaching a consensus.

"Do you think," one teacher asked, "that we should just allow the students to do whatever they like?"

"I'm not suggesting that kids play floor hockey all the time," I said, recalling reports of what had constituted gym class in our school in the past, "but I don't think most kids want to do that anyway. Over the past year I've introduced, among other things, table tennis, basketball, football, gymnastics and"—I looked reproachfully at the East Indian, Mr. Mukerjee—"yoga. And the kids enjoyed all of them; they either hadn't known they existed before or hadn't had them presented properly. The point is that a more relaxed, less competitive atmosphere makes new activities less threatening. The problem in my classes now isn't getting people to do things, it's deciding what we want to do. And that's a decision we often make as a class, or, as often as possible, individually."

"Let's remember," said Jack Gibbons, the district physical education co-ordinator, "that anything we can do to make P.E. more enjoyable and satisfying goes a long way towards convincing students that sports and physical activity can be fun, even for people who aren't particularly co-ordinated or athletically inclined."

Mr. Mukerjee looked at me. "You've used yoga in your classes?"

"Yeah. I started it this September with both my girls' and boys' classes." I decided not to mention the three students who brought notes excusing them from yoga for "religious reasons."

"I put together a booklet of basic exercises and introduced them on the mats. It was a lot of fun. Many of the kids are doing it on their own now."

"I too have used yoga," Mrs. Milord added, "and I've had very good results. And if we're talking about discipline, then let's remember that only self-discipline really lasts. Otherwise, when the threat is removed, where does the discipline go? I think yoga is a way for people to learn how to discipline themselves, how to control themselves mentally and physically. Isn't that what we really want?"

I smiled at the group ingratiatingly, hoping to weld a professional bond, and leaned forward. "Look," I said conspiratorially, "I've got to confess that for some reason I had a much harder time being open and democratic in physical education than I did, say, in English or geography. But I think that's mainly because I always had P.E. taught in a rigid, competitive, tightly teacher-controlled setting myself. I finally came to realize that if I accepted the principle that freedom and exploration were necessary for genuine intellectual growth, then it also had to apply to physical education as well."

I sat back, certain that I had made the point convincingly.

One teacher who had remained quiet during the discussion nodded slowly. "I certainly see what you are getting at," he said, "but one thing bothers me. Won't the kinds of things you're talking about be awfully hard to grade?"

As the meeting broke up for lunch, I walked quickly toward Ghislaine Milord, who was organizing her notes. Gee, I thought, as I took in her enormous brown eyes and stunning figure, she's not only right, she's beautiful.

I gave her my most winning smile. "I thought we were getting somewhere for a while there."

"I thought that all last year," she laughed. "Meeting after meeting after meeting."

We drove downtown from the high school, where the meeting was being held. "Where are you from?" I asked.

"Montreal." She pronounced it with the proper French accent.

"What are you doing here?"

165

"Well, it's a long story." Naturally. "My husband is an American, a deserter. We lived in Montreal for a couple of years while I finished university, but we wanted to get out for a while. So we wrote around, and this was the only place we could both find jobs. Peter, that's my husband, taught art last year but got fed up. So he quit."

I was intrigued. The idea of doing nothing in a Newfoundland winter seemed alluring and horrifying. "What does he do now?"

"Oh, he's working on a Local Initiatives Project, putting in a water line."

The Milords lived in Sandy Cove, a community on the Eastport peninsula (an area we had heard was especially beautiful) about fifty miles east of Gander. Ghislaine was as excited at finding Jan and me as I was at discovering her. "Come visit us," she insisted.

We needed little urging. That weekend we packed up the car and made the trip to Eastport, 110 miles from Hoberly Cove.

The only similarity between Hoberly and the Eastport district was the sea. While the land around Hoberly Cove was low, its rounded rocky ridges shaved clean by the fire, the Eastport peninsula rolled with steep wooded hills that plunged into the sea in jagged coves and inlets. A half-dozen small communities— Sandringham, Happy Adventure, Salvage, Sandy Cove, St. Chad's, Burnside—were arrayed on the edges of the penin- sula around the hub of Eastport. In summer an annual art fair drew tourists and artisans from all over North America. And every year more and more lingered, bringing with them touches of New York, Cleveland, and Toronto. It was a unique area in many ways, but in others, maybe, a harbinger of the future.

"There's not much left of the old life," Peter commented non- committally. "Outside of Salvage, which is really separated phy- sically and spiritually from the rest of the area, there aren't more than one or two full-time fishermen left on the whole peninsula."

Peter wore high boots, a stocking cap, and a flannel shirt with its sleeves rolled up to his elbows, and looked exactly like a pale version of a turn-of-the-century Quebecois lumberjack. "Why, the other day an old fella came up here to talk for a while and

166

said, 'Peter my son,'"—I was astonished at how easily and unaffectedly he slid into the dialect—"'I see you're still cutting wood for your stove. Why don't you give up that foolishness and convert to oil like the rest of us?'" The wood stove popped angrily in the corner. "It turned out I was the last person in all of Sandy Cove, excepting maybe Matt Turner, who still heated by wood. Everything's changing so fast around here it's like being caught in a time warp."

That night we talked about the special demands of living in Newfoundland. "To live here," Peter said, "you have to become a Newfoundlander, if you can. You have to cut your ties with the rest of the world." He paused. "But maybe, in the end, this place is only for those who are born here, who know the rhythms of the land and the people. Maybe," he said wistfully, "our own rootlessness prohibits us from ever adapting adequately, really accommodating."

"Maybe we just don't belong here," Jan said. "Maybe we should go away and stay away."

"Well," smiled Peter, "I've often thought the whole island should be turned into a gigantic national park. How else to preserve it? But, of course that wouldn't work either. Do you know that a brother of one of the kids I taught in school was arrested in St. John's? He'd flown in from London with eight kilos of marijuana in his baggage. And all around here the kids are only marking time till they can get out. The only people who live in this town are over forty-five and under twenty. Yet they always come back, or want to. You're born into it and it into you."

"I think," I said, slowly, "that it would have been very hard for me to have justified being here, especially as a teacher, twenty— even ten—years ago. Because we are agents of change by just living here, no doubt about it. But we're not moving into a static, tribal society now; we're in a transitional society. And the old values and institutions are under intense assault. It seems to me that the kids are growing up with a belief, fostered in part by media and mobility but also reinforced, at least tacitly, in the homes, that the traditional life style is doomed in its entirety, and good riddance. The kids are eager, desperate to forget the old ways. Toronto becomes the Emerald City, the realization of all desires."

"The tragedy is what happens when they get there," Ghislaine said, "and they find it's all a lie. They've actively rejected their past in order to find the promised fulfillment of the dream, and when it dissolves, where are they?"

I thought of Ivan, Doreen's boyfriend, shuttling restlessly between Toronto and Hoberly Cove, unable to live in either, playing drums behind strippers, dropping acid, chasing, chasing, desperately trying to be one or the other and knowing he was neither. Or Pat Whiteway, newly returned from Toronto, broke, disillusioned, listless. Or the wave of young men who left last summer for Toronto in a group—eleven at one time—some of them dropouts, others just graduated, now drifting back, bitter and uncertain.

As we left the next morning I noted Peter's cluster of firewood, drying in tall piles formed like a teepee, his buck saw hanging on the side of the house. Peter and Ghislaine grinned and waved as we trudged up the hill from their house to the road where we had parked next to their van. They, I reflected, will probably be here long after we are gone.

Back in Gander, the Integrated Studies Special Interest Committee to which I had been appointed by the superintendent had met several times that fall. At the first meeting Russell Taylor had brought us together and introduced us, then tried to give us an outline of our responsibilities. From his remarks I eventually concluded that we were being formed as a sort of loosely constucted task force on innovation in the schools, which sounded pretty good to me. For most, however, the amorphousness of the task created some anxiety, and so we embarked on a largely futile effort to "adequately define 'integration' in an educational context."

As we talked out our views, it became clear that our stumbling block was divergent philosophies rather than conflicting definitions. "I'm no God-damned psychiatrist," one man blurted out angrily after someone had suggested integrating the learning in the schools with the lives of the students, thereby better meeting their emotional and educational needs. "I don't know what these kids' 'emotional needs' are, and I don't much care. I'm a teacher."

In the end, however, the majority of us agreed that a mere mechanical combination of subjects was not enough; somehow we had to focus on the broader issue of how to attack the fundamental problem. This was—as Howard Green, a teacher from Dover, put it—that "our schools are boring, inflexible and irrelevant. And," he growled, "I'll be damned if I'm going to waste my time on another committee that accomplishes nothing." I liked his attitude.

The lack of homogeneity was not, we found, a real problem after all. By the third or fourth meeting, those who attended the sessions had dwindled to about six, with only four of us really committed. Besides myself there was Howard (who was yet another American, I discovered, teaching with his wife for their second year in Dover), Ed Randall, principal of a small elementary school, and Jack Ryan, vice-principal of the Dark Cove high school. We soon found that despite our unanimity in desiring to make a strong statement, we were unable to arrive at a format that would have any influence.

"No matter how many recommendations we make based on whatever data," Jack said, "our eventual report will remain totally ignored. What teachers or administrators are going to listen to a four-man committee made up of people from the lunatic fringe? They don't even listen to the superintendent."

"Maybe," I suggested, only half seriously, "since we're talking about educational change we might try something unheard of and ask the victims, uh, recipients of the present system about what changes they'd like to see."

"That's it!" Howard shouted. "A student conference on education. We'll bring in students from all the high schools in the district sometime in the spring, help them organize a conference, have them draw up some recommendations based on their discussions and compile them into a report."

It was already November when we came up with the concept, and the logistics, even assuming we could wrangle the co-operation of the central office and the various principals, seemed immense. For example, Fogo Island was already cut off by ice. How would we get students from the high school there into Gander? By air? Still, problems notwithstanding, we were ecstatic. For the first time in Newfoundland (in Canada?) a conference of students from an entire school district would convene to articulate and assemble a set of recommendations for students and administrators alike. Maybe nothing would come of it other than a few somewhat more aware students, but it was clearly the most positive statement our committee could make. Not about specific changes, perhaps, but about who should be the first considered, and consulted, in any educational changes.

Though school progressed predictably for Jan and me, we both began to feel a sort of growing desperation, a mounting impatience with the subtle restraints built into the structure which we were constantly bumping our heads against. Even those breakthroughs that occurred—like Jan's success in bringing parents into the classroom—only seemed to underscore the immensity of the web of indifference and inertia that gripped the schools.

Films continued to engender excitement and discussion. *The Best Damn Fiddler from Calaboogie to Kaladar* was the story of a family in rural Ontario trying to hold onto their old life style despite the pressures of poverty—and the restless inability of the oldest daughter, played by Margot Kidder, to accept her parents' world.

The movie was so moving and pertinent that I decided to show it to the entire community, for a donation of twenty-five cents that would go to the library fund. The town was starved for entertainment. Every chair was filled and people sat on the floor, more than three hundred in all.

I was a little nervous. In one scene, while getting ready for a party, Margot Kidder slips off her sweater and snaps on a bra, providing the audience with a fleeting glimpse of one breast. Uncertain about community standards, I decided to see Norman about it. He snorted. "Most of these kids live in small houses with large families. I don't think seeing a woman's breast on the screen will upset anyone." I was as surprised by his reaction as the crowd's—there was not a ripple, nor were there any complaints later.

Nonetheless, sex education remained a very touchy issue. There was a degree of tolerance of sexual activity in the community, but there was also a tremendous amount of ignorance and misinformation, evidenced by the number of young girls who became pregnant each year and dropped out of school. From talking with the kids I concluded that there was substantially more sexual activity than knowledge. There seemed to be almost no dialogue in the homes, and the kids felt they had no place to turn for information or advice. The sexual encounters themselves seemed pretty furtive; parents did not condone sex, they just ignored it, so in a town with a few cars, cold weather and no homes available, trysts occurred between young people—who were often confused and unprepared to handle the emotional implications of their action—often in pretty uncomfortable surroundings.

Despite the results of the sex education questionnaire and my own inquiries, however, no one was willing to take the first step; no sex education program of any sort was on the horizon. In class, sexual themes had been dealt with obliquely almost from the beginning, but the film *Phoebe*, the story of a girl who becomes pregnant while in high school, led us to focus on the subject. There was no embarrassment among the kids, just interest. One boy commented, "It's too bad she had to get pregnant." A girl asked timidly what abortion was—she had heard the term but was unclear what it meant.

Through the *Psychology Today* book club I had received a book called *The Sex Book* which the kids who had come up to the house found fascinating. The text was a series of clear, concise definitions of sexual terms and concepts listed in dictionary form. The accompanying illustrations were explicit pictures of the sexual organs, couples making love, naked children and families and people exploring their own bodies. But the candour and tone of the pictures brought the whole to a level of openness and naturalness that was neither threatening nor titillating.

171

On the first two pages of the book, there is reproduced a series of cards with handwritten questions from young people. I found the anonymous question technique immensely appealing for my own situation. As obvious as it was, it allowed the genuine concerns of young people to be heard. I saw that if discussion were to be based on such questions, the information provided would be immediately salient—not too abstract or formal, not too sophisticated or simple.

I brought the book into my grade nine class and passed out small squares of paper, explaining that I wanted the students to write down whatever questions about sex they would like answered. I would then go to the book, read the appropriate sections, and discuss the question further with the class as a whole. The questions revealed a great deal:

"What age does a girl begin her period and how long does she have it?"

"Why do so many young people think sex is dirty?"

"What is the best birth control method?"

"Why are girls more highly condemned for having sexual intercourse before marriage than boys?"

"Why do they use birth control pills?"

"Do males or females need sex more?"

"Do you think making love is harmful?"

"Can one know if he is in love without having sexual intercourse?"

"How much sperm does a man have? Can he lose it?"

"Where can you get birth control pills?"

"Is circumcision necessary?"

"What is a bugger?"

"Is masturbation a desire for the opposite sex?"

"Why do people masturbate?"

"Do you think sex is a good thing?"

"Do girls enjoy sex as much as men?"

"Is sex before marriage morally wrong?"

"Can a girl get pregnant when a man screws her but doesn't come in her?"

"Is a safe any good?"

172

"What exactly is an abortion? Why do so many people disagree with it?"

"Do you think sex should be taught in school and at home?"

"How are twins developed?"

We spent several periods in discussion, everyone respectful of each other and genuinely interested. Finally, after we had talked through most of the questions, one student raised his hand.

"Mr. Sawyer, can we look at that book?"

What to do? Up to this point the class had remained tied to the concerns of the kids, and discussion had been maintained at a level I hoped would not antagonize the parents. Now I was being asked to open the book, with its uncompromisingly frank pictures, to the class. I had little doubt that the content of the pictures would be seen as indecent by many of the parents, but on the other hand if I refused I would simply be reinforcing the feelings of guilt that had already accompanied much of these kids' sexual training. If I believed that sex should be dealt with openly, how could I now refuse? No explanation would be sufficient to erase the feeling that once more sex had been deemed dirty and secret, too shameful to be fully scrutinized.

Still, how long would I last as a teacher here if I did let them look?

"Well, I'll tell you what." I was desperately trying to come up with a solution. "I'll leave the book on the table and if anyone wants to look at it, he or she can." A few boys had already leapt from their seats. I motioned them back. "But, if you don't want to look at it that's absolutely up to you." It was the best I could do under the circumstances.

A cluster of boys gathered around the table, and again I was amazed by their maturity. Only one boy snickered once, and he was quickly glowered into silence. More drifted up as others went back to their seats. Finally, after the boys had finished, one girl stood up resolutely and marched for the table. Before she got there, she had been joined by half the other girls. They too leafed seriously through the book, reading occasional entries and inspecting the pictures. After a while, they sat down and I was left alone with the book, imagining the outraged parents converging on the school, screaming for my blood.

The storm never came. I eventually realized that the kids were not stupid. They understood what the repercussions could be. And since they had enjoyed the sessions and appreciated them, there was no reason for them to report it in a manner that would raise their parents' ire. My faith in the kids and respect for their judgement increased even further.

In early December, Jan came home upset and shaken. "Do you remember when I told you the dentist was coming to school and that I wanted him to look at Clayton's teeth?" I nodded. Clayton was one of Jan's students who had two rows of upper and lower front teeth, the extra teeth producing, among other things, a speech impediment. "Well, he wasn't in school yesterday when the dentist came. But today he came back and," her voice almost broke, "his father had pulled out the teeth himself with pliers. Poor Clayton. He was in so much pain and his gums kept bleeding, so I finally took him over to the nurse."

Though perhaps the most pathetic, this was not the first case of that sort we had encountered. Isolated and ignored, rural Newfoundlanders had long been forced to rely on their own health-care devices and medicines. Even now, we were told, Newfoundland had the worst physician-to-population ratio in any province, territory or state in North America. And the quality of the physicians attracted to Newfoundland was mixed at best. They were too often lured by the chance for immense salaries and low standards, both necessitated by the province's critical shortage of medical personnel.

The provincial government, by establishing a medical school in St. John's and instituting full scholarships in return for two years service at the government's discretion, was approaching the problem, but with mixed success. The inaccessibility of many communities, traditional roles, and the continued failings of the public school system hampered progress. One girl in my grade eleven class, a brilliant, extremely capable young woman, was intent on becoming a nurse. "Look," I said in exasperation one day, "why not become a doctor if you're interested in medicine?"

174

Sarah laughed uneasily. "Well, you know. Girls don't become doctors, just nurses."

It seemed clear that despite government programs the bulk of medical personnel would continue to come from outside the province for the foreseeable future. In the cities, where working conditions were good, life was relatively comfortable and where they were subjected to scrutiny, the problem was not particularly serious: doctors, from whatever source, were generally competent, professional and ethical. But in the outports, usually served by a public health nurse or a freelance physician and a regional cottage hospital (often located fifty, sixty or more miles from the community) the situation was different.

Many of the physicians operating in these areas held questionable credentials and had received limited training. Only a small percentage were accredited by the provincial government, yet, because of the difficulty in luring qualified people, they were allowed to practise. Even more damaging, perhaps, than their limited skills was a contempt many of them seemed to hold for Newfoundlanders. For example, when Judy Davies went to the Northport dentist, who had come from Britain some twelve years before and had since made a fortune, he clucked with concern after examining her teeth. "You've got a pretty large cavity in one tooth," he told her. "If you were a Newfie I'd pull it, but as you're not I'll go ahead and fill it."

I encountered the most outrageous example of arrogance and medical incompetence, bordering on the criminal, in a doctor who had located in a nearby community years before we arrived. I first heard of him when a friend's son had visited the garden the previous spring with his arm in a sling. He had fallen off his motorcycle while riding it near Northport, dislocating his shoulder, and had been carried in to this man.

"He had me lie on a cot. Then he put his foot in my armpit, grabbed my hand and yanked as hard as he could." Patrick's eyes clouded at the memory. "It was the most God-awful pain I've ever experienced in my life."

"You mean he didn't use any anesthetic?"

"Nothing at all. I went up to the hospital and let Dr. Lee look at it." Dr. Lee was the extraordinarily capable Chinese doctor at

Warrendale who was respected by everyone in the area. "He shook his head and said it was the most barbaric treatment he'd ever heard of, but at least it's back in place. He said that this guy could have torn the ligaments beyond repair, but apparently he didn't."

The rumour was that this European doctor, since he was the sole distributor for drugs in the area, routinely prescribed addictive doses of antidepressants and pain pills, usually for no reason other than the steady income the drug sales provided. "Sure," Norman confirmed, "everyone knows about it. He especially does it with older people. But what can you do? They won't complain and it's impossible to prove anything. He just claims medical judgement."

One night I found myself sitting across from this doctor in a tavern. At first I ignored him, but after a few beers I leaned across the table. "I understand you're a doctor. How long have you been here?"

He looked at me shrewdly. "Three years. Can you imagine that? I've been in this damned place for three years. Where are you from?"

"Originally I'm from the States."

"Well, then," he waved his hand as if no more explanation were required, "you can see why I hate this place so much. And the people! No concept of culture, nothing. They possess no sense of beauty. It's like working with animals."

I could feel the adrenalin surge through my body. "So you come here," I said, my voice beginning to break with anger, "and suck these people's blood, steal enough money from them to return to Europe and live comfortably with people who aren't so coarse and insensitive? It must be a real ordeal for you to have to live with people who are so hopelessly subhuman."

"Ah!" he spat out in disgust. "You're an American. What do you know? Don't let anyone tell you differently; some races are genetically superior to others. Newfoundlanders are simply an inferior people. What have they written?" He snickered. "Most of them can't even write. Where are their architectural or artistic accomplishments? My people, on the other hand, have proven historically their supremacy."

The blood was pumping into my head and when I spoke my voice, tight and gritty, didn't sound like mine. "You're right. I don't know a lot about your country. But I know that anyone who would give an ignorant, bigoted swine like you a licence to practise medicine must be as much of a moron as you are."

I sat tense and poised, my hands clenched on the table. Around us, silence had descended. His eyes flickered and darted. Finally he snorted derisively, pushed his chair back and walked to another table. He left the tavern soon after.

I never saw him again. That spring he left for home, and certainly no one mourned his leaving.

The most horrible tales of a medical nature came from a young woman in the community who had worked as a public health nurse in another part of the island. She finally quit, she told us, when she could no longer work with the only physician.

"He was an alcoholic," she confided, "and yet the government sent him to be responsible for the health care of the entire place, can you imagine that? The final straw was the day he did a varicose vein operation on a woman.

"She was scared stiff to begin with, you know, but he assured her that the operation would be painless. He'd scheduled the thing for 2:00 in the afternoon, so I administered the local anesthetic around 1:30. She lay there and lay there, getting more upset all the time. Well, he finally came in about 5:00, absolutely loaded. He told me to get the instruments ready, and when I suggested he hold off he took a swing at me. If it wasn't for the woman I'd have walked out right then.

"By this time the anesthetic had largely worn off, but he wouldn't hear it. He picked up a scalpel and started slicing. Blood was everywhere. He was too drunk to tie off the veins, so I tried to do it while he cut. The woman was nearly hysterical with pain and fear. 'What's the matter,' he snarled at her. 'Can't you take it?' Finally he gave up. He lurched out the door after more liquor, ordering me to keep the woman on the table.

"She was still whimpering and her leg was a bloody mess. I managed to finish tying off the veins and clean her up and close the incisions. Then I tried to calm her enough to move her. I got her leg bandaged and moved her out of the clinic. When the doctor came back, even drunker, he was enraged. He chased me around the room, screaming at the top of his lungs. I locked myself into the office and listened to him curse and throw things around the operating room. Finally he stomped out."

"What happened to him?" Jan exclaimed, totally horrified.

"Well, I wrote the medical board and explained why I was resigning. It wasn't the first time this guy had done something like that. So, last time I heard he'd been reassigned. But he's probably still practising somewhere."

December crept up on us unnoticed. This year we had managed to acclimatize ourselves to the extent that we were at least not paralyzed by the cold and snow. We often drove down the thickly frozen Rocky Bay River on Saturdays, along with a good portion of the rest of the town, to where men from Hoberly Cove had been cutting firewood. Here, miles from the bridge in country virtually inaccessible during the summer, cars and pick-ups were lined up on the ice like a parking lot and campfires crackled on the shores. People ate lunch, talked and strolled from group to group, usually to the accompaniment of distant chain saws.

One day after a heavy snowfall, I heard a clunking and glanced out our window to see a caterpillar tractor grunting and wheezing up the narrow lane between our house and Morgan's. To my astonishment I saw that, just barely clearing the fences on each side of it, was a house being pulled on skids.

I remembered Morgan mentioning the house months before. He had built it ten years ago but had never lived in it, buying instead the small house they now lived in for the adjacent garage and the location. Now he had decided it was time to bring the house to the lot, a not unusual occurrence in a town where money and timber were scarce.

"We used to move them by men and horses years ago," he explained later, almost as if to apologize for the noisy caterpillar. "Why, when Charlie Pritchett moved his house from Rocky Bay to Hoberly we jacked it up, fit skids underneath, hitched up a few horses and hauled it all the way to the harbour. His wife washed dishes the whole way."

We had decided long ago to stay in Hoberly Cove for the holidays and were actually looking forward to a Christmas on our own, away from our families. Around the middle of the month Warrick, Maxwell, Benjamin and Kevin took me out to look for a Christmas tree. We walked into a thick copse of fir and found a perfectly formed tree. Max and Warrick both insisted on hacking it down and somehow managed to do so without lopping off the other's fingers. We dragged it to the road, tied it onto the SAAB, and hauled it back home, where we posed on the back bridge holding the tree while Jan snapped pictures.

Christmas itself did not start out well. After we had opened our gifts we sat quietly on the rug and, for the first time in weeks, felt alone. But the quiet did not last long. Just about the time we had started to work up a good case of melancholia, we heard boots clump up the back stairs.

"Merry Christmas," Benjamin Collins said as I opened the back door. "My mother sent up a few little things," he mumbled almost shyly, holding up a large package in his mitted hands.

Ben came in while we opened the box. His mother, who was always protesting that Benjamin was up at the house too much and was eating us into bankruptcy, had sent a whole marshberry tart, a loaf of bread, three jars of salmon and an enormous moose roast. Soon other kids filed up, filling the house with laughter, noise and whizzing darts. In the afternoon Roger and Judy and their new baby came for dinner, and later, after everyone had gone home, Morgan stopped over with more fresh-baked bread and a dozen beers. "I'd have come over sooner," he said, "but the place was always full of young'uns. I've got enough of them at my house." It was, I realized, becoming harder and harder to get lonely.

But late that night after the last visitor had left, we sat quietly on the couch, very close to each other, and watched the snow fall silently outside our window.

11

"The fact that a man has wrenches doesn't make him a good mechanic"

It was a Sunday night in late February, and Jan and I sat with Howard and Christy Green in the lounge of Gander's Albatross Motel, an increasingly frequent Sunday night ritual. Since we had got to know Howard and Christy through the Integrated Studies Special Interest Committee, we had become friends, visiting each other occasionally. They taught ninety miles away and normally we met in Gander for dinner. Lately we had found ourselves clinging to each other's company more fiercely, often staying in Gander until ridiculous hours, despite knowing we had a two-hour return trip ahead through the winter night.

Dover, where Howard and Christy taught, was as similar physically to Hoberly Cove as Sandy Cove had been different. Dover lay across the peninsula from Hoberly Cove on an arm from Bonavista Bay and shared the same low, rocky, fire-blackened topography. But socially and economically the situation there was considerably worse. The economy of the northwest coast of Bonavista Bay had traditionally been based on fishing and forestry and had been the centre of the IWA union struggle to organize the pulp wood cutters a decade before. With the destruction of the forests and collapse of the fisheries, which had deteriorated more rapidly in the area than around Hoberly Cove, the region had been economically and psychologically devastated. The ill-conceived and often misadministered relocation program of the '50s had not alleviated the problems by moving people in from the islands to the mainland communities without being able to provide employment or decent facilities. In Dover, Howard had told me, ninety per cent of the people were totally dependent on welfare.

"Look, it's real simple," he had replied to my exclamation of disbelief. "The only reason these communities are located where they are was fishing. It was the sole economic base, the only possible source of income. There is no possibility of manufacturing industry ever locating there, and other primary industries, especially logging now, are unfeasible. Relocation in larger centres isn't the answer—there aren't enough jobs for the people living in the towns now. So we're left with people who have always worked incredibly hard, trapped in their communities with nothing to do and little hope of anything developing. Not because they want to be on welfare, but because historical accident and government bungling have conspired to destroy the only way of life that could support their communities."

I found in Howard a much needed friend and confidant, someone to share educational tactics and political observations with. In Christy, who taught junior secondary grades, Jan found a woman with similar experiences and perceptions to whom she could voice her anxieties. They provided each other with the support they both desperately needed.

By Easter we had become so close that we took a trip together around the Burin Peninsula, a trip that led to an exciting dream which, for a moment, looked as if it might become a reality. Halfway through Terra Nova National Park on our way to Burin we saw a sign that pointed inland to the community of Terra Nova. It was a place that I had wanted to see. What kind of town would be located fifteen miles inland from such a point? We negotiated the dirt road and, bouncing over a last rise, curved right and looked over the town of Terra Nova. It was an unusual community for Newfoundland, as it had obviously been laid out along the railroad, strung out for half a mile on each side. All around the community were the low wooded hills typical of the interior of this area.

Empty buildings were everywhere. Dozens of homes had been closed and abandoned. Stores, some with stock still in the windows, were padlocked and dark. Even churches and one large school were empty and unused. Two huge warehouses sat closed and deserted at the northern end of town. Only a small new cement-block school with cut-out pictures of rabbits and flowers on the windows showed that life went on somewhere.

After winding through the streets we eventually found a general store and restaurant which was partially open. The back section had been closed and was heaped with empty boxes and stacked chairs and tables. Only a counter remained usable.

A man looked at us in surprise as we walked in. It turned out that he, too, was in the process of leaving. "I've lived here fifteen years, but I sure can't make a living any more. Guess I'll just shut it all up and try to find something in Gander." The town, he told us, had grown up around the pine forests that had once been thick in the region. When that had been cut out, the town began to die. "The final blow was the discontinuation of the passenger trains," he said. "One of those big buildings at the north end was used to service passenger and freight cars. When they discontinued the passenger service they moved everything to Grand Falls. The other building was a warehouse used to store lumber for loading. Neither one has been used for nearly six years now."

As we drove out of town, Howard mused quietly, "What a great place for an alternative school."

I seized on the idea enthusiastically. "Sure! The Terra Nova School. It's got all the buildings already here. We could convert the warehouse into a gym, the old school into the learning centre, the restaurant into a cafeteria." Before long I was reeling off all the possibilities. "Kids could live in the houses, really integrating living with learning. The whole place could become a campus. We've got immediate access to the country for science

182

and outdoor education. Part of the whole experience would be to renovate the place. The students would essentially build their own school. It's in our board, so they might be willing to support us as an alternative for some kids from throughout the district that can't adapt to regular schools. It's got everything."

"Except the community," Howard pointed out. "As we've said before, one of the big problems now with the schools is that they're too far removed from the community, right? So wouldn't a residential school like this further separate the school from the larger community?"

I paused. "I don't know. First of all we'd only take kids who wanted to come and whose parents agreed and supported the school. Second, we'd be creating a new community in the town. There are probably still enough families living here so we wouldn't become totally isolated."

"Maybe," Howard agreed. "Probably only St. John's and Corner Brook are capable of supporting an alternative school within the community. Perhaps the only answer for the time being is to set up a central alternative school for a district and bring the kids to the school. After the approaches and techniques have been worked out and demonstrated we might then be able to bring those innovations back into the regular schools with less opposition."

Christy, who was set on leaving the island, was alarmed. "What about equipment? You wouldn't have any learning materials."

"Between the four of us we have more audio visual equipment now, with the exception of a projector, than our whole high school," I said. "With our books and three hundred dollars we could put together a better library than you'll find in ninety per cent of outport high schools today. And the buildings available here would provide better facilities, both operationally and structurally, than what we're now working in. There would be room for small groups, individual work, large groups. And look, there are gardens in our backyard. We could build greenhouses, raise animals, teach practical agriculture, carpentry, bricklaying—the things the community used to teach. The possibilities are endless."

183

I realized my enthusiasm was soaring above the massive physical and philosophical problems such an operation would actually entail, but the thought of creating a living educational community of students and educators in a rich, flexible setting was too exciting to abandon easily.

"It would be an attempt to redefine school," I continued. "Why are these kids in school now? Largely because they're coerced into being there. What do they have to look forward to? Deferred gratification in the form of a "good job" when they get out, jobs which are unavailable in their communities when they leave anyway. What would happen if students and teachers came together not for grades or money or future payoffs but because the experience was enjoyable and satisfying now? Just think of the implications! Think of just the different attitudes towards learning it would produce."

As we travelled we thought excitedly about Terra Nova's possibilities, and after our return we pursued our idea in earnest. Although it was received with a surprising amount of sympathy, we were offered little outright support. We knew that an army of enthusiasts would be needed to organize such an operation. Without practical encouragement, and given Christy's determination to leave Newfoundland, we reluctantly abandoned the project.

Meanwhile preparations for the student conference to be held in March had progressed well. We had approached Russell Taylor with the idea in November and he had supported the venture warmly. "I didn't know what you guys would come up with," he said, "but I figured it would be interesting."

Securing support from the nine high schools was touchier. Many principals treated the idea coolly and demanded explanations and assurances. Some grumbled about the time students would be missing ("These kids have to spend every day in class if they hope to get through the material," one commented), and others seemed alarmed at the idea of students meeting together for the purpose of discussing educational change. They seemed to take the attitude that, as professionals, teachers needed no help in making decisions about the operation of schools, and certainly not from students.

184

We sent out a packet of materials to each high school, trying to explain the purpose of the conference in language that was as non-inflammatory as possible. The conference, we wrote, "would for the first time draw students from all over the board to discuss among themselves their ideas on education and the direction they would like to see it move in. The focus of the conference will be 'The Student's Role in Shaping Education for the Future.' We expect the results will allow teachers and administrators to better assess student views and needs." We also sent along a discussion paper based loosely on my first Deep Thought Quiz, and copies of eight student-developed "possible discussion topics": (1) student rights and student power; (2) change in the traditional role of the teacher in the classroom and his relationship with students; (3) curriculum; (4) what do students want out of education? What is education?; (5) evaluation and testing; (6) changes in the physical structure of the school; (7) teacher qualifications; and (8) making what is taught in school more relevant to the needs of the students.

We also set a date in late March for the gathering. We asked for three to five students from each school and eventually, often with some reluctance, received indications of some sort of cooperation from each.

Before the big conference, however, we had the opportunity to try out the idea in Hoberly Cove. Education Week was an annual occurrence in Newfoundland that usually produced a few posters exhorting students to stay in school, and little else. This year, however, with the theme "Education is Living," the kids in our high school said they wanted to do something really different. We set out to make the week of March 7 to 13 exceptional by planning a full program, including a small-scale student conference.

On Monday we held field day—a first for Hoberly Cove—where classes competed in such events as the egg throw, tug-of-war, sack races, sprints and relays. Wednesday was entirely devoted to a hike. The whole school clambered onto the two buses in the community and travelled to a rendezvous point about twelve miles west of town. From there, most of the grade nines and I struck out for a high rock formation several miles away. Eventually, leaving a few students at a campfire en route, about twenty of us worked our way to the lower end of the flat, tilted top of the curious formation. While the surrounding country was low and rolling, the hill we were on jutted up from the ponds below like an enormous loaf of bread. After catching our breath, we walked upwards towards the far rim, about half a mile away, which formed the peak. Midway we discovered a perfectly round pond of clear ice surrounded by boulders that seemed to be evenly placed around the perimeter of the pond. There was a strange, almost mystical feeling about the place, and we stopped and sat quietly on the rocks.

"I've heard about this place," one boy said. "My father told me that this used to be where the Indians held ceremonies when they came to this area in the spring."

An even deeper quiet spread over the bare, wind-swept plateau. The Beothucks, the nomadic native people of Newfoundland, had hunted and fished in this area for hundreds of years, until they were finally completely wiped out in the early nineteenth century. One boy had once confided in class that his great-great-great grandfather had killed the last Indian on the straight shore. "He was hunting birds and saw this Indian on the beach with three birds hanging from his belt. So he shot the Indian and took the birds."

A sort of national shame seemed burned into the Newfoundland conscience over the early settlers' treatment of the Beothucks. People would mention with chagrin how one man had once been elected magistrate in Twillingate on the strength of having killed forty Indians, though the Beothucks seldom if ever harmed a white man, woman or child. They may have numbered about five hundred at the time of the first contact with the white man, but by 1800 the systematic extermination campaign of the fearful fishermen, who resented the Indians' petty thefts of gear and ignored or misunderstood the beads and strips of cloth left in payment, had nearly wiped them out. As if this pressure was not enough, the French offered a bounty for Beothuck scalps; later, Micmacs from Nova Scotia, lured by the promise of Beothuck

186

land, were brought onto the island to continue the relentless hunt.

In 1819 the last band of natives were persuaded to surrender "for their own preservation." When they emerged from the forest to throw themselves on the mercy of the crown, either treachery or nervousness caused one of the white men to misinterpret a sign of peace as a gesture of hostility, and he shot into the tiny band of unarmed Indians. By the time the shooting was over, most of the remaining Beothucks lay dead, and the handful who escaped died in the forest in terrible loneliness. The last Beothuck was Shawnawdithit, the wife of the slain Beothuck chief, who was captured and worked as a maid until she died in 1829, taking with her the language, history and culture of an entire people.

The kids seemed to feel the horror of the genocide story most acutely. Now they sat listening to the wind moan around the rocks and looked into the frozen surface of the tiny pool.

We continued along the stony, broken surface of the flat hill top and finally reached the summit. We could see the blue water of Hamilton Sound to the west and the endless expanse of green-blotched white terrain on each side. In the distance we could just make out the winding Rocky Bay River, and far away we could see the yellow school buses and an occasional tiny figure moving around the fires.

We had found a tall, weathered spruce trunk on the way up and had dragged it with us up the hill. Now we made a cairn of stones to set it in, and Warrick donated an old stocking cap which we tied to the top like an pennant. We braced the pole firmly against the constant wind and began to make our way back through the snow and rock to the ground below.

When we left that afternoon on the bus, a ninth grader yelled to me and pointed out the window. There, snapping smartly in the wind, was Warrick's much mended orange hat, small but distinct, flying high atop the hill we had conquered.

Other activities of Education Week proceeded with mixed success: parents' night, a discussion of fishing in Hoberly Cove, visits to a town council meeting, a talent show, and an afternoon open house. The two major events remaining were the student conference on Thursday and the dance, to be held in the Orange Lodge, scheduled for Saturday night.

I saw the Squire Memorial High School student conference as a sort of test run for the Gander conference to be held two weeks later. Because of this I watched its progress very closely, and was delighted. The students had earlier drawn up a list of eight areas of discussion—we borrowed it for the Gander conference—and these provided the basis for the morning's talks. A panel discussion open to the public took up the afternoon. A report, later written, typed, reproduced and distributed by the students, summed up the day:

"On March 9th students from Thornton Central High, Rockwood High, Centennial High and Squire Memorial High met in the auditorium of S.M.H. for a student conference. As far as we know it was the first ever held in Newfoundland with the students presenting their ideas on the future of education. There were no teachers present and everything was run by the students. It was important to stress that everything went very smoothly, with everyone co-operating and participating in the group discussion.

"On the morning of the conference we had everyone register and become acquainted with each other. We also passed out handout sheets and an agenda at that time.

"After the opening address the students split into five different groups with a student from a different school in each group. These groups discussed various topics they thought were important. It seemed all the ideas presented focussed on change, which was appropriate since the title of the conference was: 'Students and the Future of Education: Focus on Change.'"

The report reviewed the ideas that had emerged from the discussions. "We need a student union that has power and can vote on an issue." Another approach, they thought, was "to have student representatives at the school board meetings so they could find out what was going on and bring it back to the students." They felt that public exams should be done away with and students marked on "progress and effort." They wanted independent study rooms, and maybe even no seats, just carpeting in some rooms "so people might feel more comfortable and probably communicate better with each other." But "a lot depends on the students as well as other people involved."

They were not happy with teachers' roles; they felt that teachers should act more as helpers, allowing students to work at their own speed, making them "more independent and responsible." "Today," they commented, "whether we care to admit it or not, the teachers are considered superior to students." This relationship should be changed, they said, to one based on friendship. "The teacher is really a student's friend but most everyone seems to be moulded to think a teacher is someone a student is afraid of and dislikes. Really we like the teachers, but we think we're not supposed to because they're teachers."

The report also commented that students wanted courses which were "more useful to students after they leave school" with a wider variety of course options, and that a teacher should be "paid according to his ability to teach and by his achievements with the students, not by the number of degrees he has."

In the afternoon the panel of students from each of the schools was formed to present and discuss the ideas developed during the morning session. Teachers, students and parents were invited to participate, and the gym was crowded for the discussion. The panel members sat at a long table on the stage. Essentially they reviewed the main points of the report, handling questions from each other and the audience. All went smoothly, until the students brought up the idea of paying teachers according to their teaching ability.

"Come, come," one teacher said from the audience, "who could determine something as subjective as a teacher's ability?"

Linda Collins, the chairperson, spoke unhesitatingly. "The students, of course. You judge our ability all the time."

Another teacher spoke from the floor. "This sounds very nice," he explained patiently, "but you're forgetting that to be good, a teacher must have the tools, not necessarily be liked. Certificates and teacher training insure that teachers possess the proper tools to get the job done, just like a mechanic must have wrenches to do his job."

Warrick Pike, who was now in the audience, stood up by the

far wall. "Sure, a mechanic needs wrenches to do a good job, but the fact that a man has wrenches doesn't make him a good mechanic. Any bloody old fool can buy a set of wrenches, but that sure doesn't mean he knows what to do with them." The audience went wild applauding Warrick, stomping and hooting their approval.

All the students agreed that the conference had been a success. The report was run off and twenty-five copies sent to each school. "We are all looking forward to taking part in other conferences like this one," they concluded.

The final event of Hoberly Cove's Education Week was Saturday night's dance. The Orange Lodge was picked for the site because the school was still prohibited from holding dances and the larger United Church hall had been condemned.

The origins of the Orange Lodge lay in the struggles between Protestant and Catholic factions in Ireland when the Orangemen formed the militantly Protestant, British-oriented order to combat the rising tide of Irish Catholic nationalism. In Newfoundland, the struggle had been continued as the island was settled by Irishmen of both factions. One clash in the 1800s in the town of Harbour Grace had killed a dozen men, and an engraving of the battle, draped with an orange sash worn by a combatant, hung prominently in the Hoberly Cove hall. But those days had been more or less forgotten. Now the organization served as a kind of secret club for men.

The hall was little larger than a big living room, heated by a single wood stove in the middle of the floor. With a slightly raised platform in the front and large side windows it seemed like a church without pews. The band too, left something to be desired, being made up of mostly local musicians possessing varying degrees of skill. But the kids, starved for a dance of any kind, seemed oblivious to the music's shortcomings and danced until they were soaked with perspiration.

On the day of the Gander district-wide student conference, I left Hoberly Cove at 5:30 in the morning—the five students from our school drove in later with Calvin Sturge—and arrived at the school board office to find Jack and Ed already there and working.

190

Howard walked up, carrying a ream of paper. "By the way, Russell and the central office staff want to meet with the student reps today."

"Oh. Isn't that O.K.?"

"I suppose, but I'm not crazy about the idea. The whole point of the conference was that the kids would have the opportunity to discuss freely without any outside interference. You know the staff will tend to overpower the kids and redirect them."

"Well, if Hoberly Cove is any example, the kids can stand up pretty well for what they think."

By the time the groups of students began to arrive, we had managed to organize a coffee urn, check that the conference room was set up and ready, clear rights to the duplicator for the agenda that a steering committee would draw up, and make arrangements for forty box lunches. We asked an early student to act as registrar and armed him with a stack of name tags.

By 8:30 almost all of the school reps were present; they quickly elected as their chairman an eleventh grader from Hoberly Cove, Paul Pritchett, and selected a steering committee. While the rest of the students mixed easily, drinking coffee and talking, Paul and his steering committee worked out an agenda. It was ready in ten minutes and was very similar to the format followed in Hoberly Cove, except that the final panel was to be held before the central office staff instead of a general audience.

One thing we teachers had learned from the Hoberly conference was that students were at least as capable of running a conference effectively as we were. So, having done the preliminary work by supplying them with recorders, paper and other materials, we closed the doors to the conference room and retreated.

By noon it was clear that things were going very well. The kids left the conference room beaming and talking warmly with students they had met only a few hours before. The cassettes were filled with hours of discussion. After a lunch of take-out food, they went back to work. We were hoping that the session would produce a document of specific recommendations, but by the time Russell and the rest of the staff appeared, marking the end of the work sessions, we were left with only masses of notes and

191

taped conversations and nine general recommendations.

"We were in the process of writing up more detailed remarks when we ran out of time," Paul said ruefully. "But I think everything we need is in there, somewhere."

"O.K., Paul," I sighed. "You did an excellent job. I guess we'll try to put it all together from the notes and tapes, then I'll show it to you for your approval before we release it."

We spent all that night and the next three meetings listening to the tapes of the discussions and working through the thirty pages of notes. We finally put together a report which we felt accurately represented the tone and content of the conference. Paul and the rest of the steering committee approved the document enthusiastically and we printed up 2,300 copies, enough for every student and teacher in nine high schools in the district.

What students wanted out of education, the report said, was "a good future and something that helps us understand our problems and someone else's." At the same time they recognized that "each person has different meanings of education and wants different things from it." In any case, they said, de-emphasis on academic performance would help everyone. "A person should be evaluated by his effort, progress and his ability to get along with other people, not by a stupid percentage. There shouldn't be any particular percentage or average tagged on a person; let people work at their own level. . . . " They wanted public exams scrapped. "Public exams are not a fair judgement of a person's character or ability," they said.

The delegates reaffirmed that they wanted greater control over the decisions that affected their educational life and demanded greater freedom in using facilities, choosing their classes, conducting their classes and expressing their ideas. One of the comments made was that "students should have freedom, but they should get it from grade one so they'll know how to use it."

The Gander delegates came out particularly strongly for a student union. They suggested that representatives should come from each school to form the executive and the local unions would then function in each high school to deal with local grievances. General meetings would be held monthly. One small group developed a detailed proposal for organizing such a body that seemed remarkably sophisticated and workable.

The general attitude towards teachers was that students wanted them to be more humane. The students wanted "a closer relationship" that was "free of fear and tension" and wanted the teacher to operate more as an advisor and reference person. "As it is now," they stated, "a student's failure is often more the fault of the teacher than the student. In life if a man shags up his work then he is a failure, but if a teacher messes up his job, then the students that he taught are considered failures." They listed five specifics a teacher should be: (1) able to get along with his students; (2) open-minded; (3) able to accept other people's views; (4) paid for his ability to teach; and (5) able to get his ideas across to the student.

Many, working daily in facilities at least as stark and poorly equipped as Squire Memorial, were upset about the physical structures of the school. "Make the classroom more comfortable and informal," they pleaded, "and provide facilities for a greater variety of activity." Specifically they wanted a student lounge "where students can smoke, relax and discuss"; independent study rooms; tables instead of desks; movable partitions; better lab facilities; better, higher, more flexible gyms, and more carpeted areas.

The curriculum changes they wanted centred around increased choice and relevancy to their own lives. As "new" electives that they wanted to see they listed navigation, driver education, sex education, both home economics and industrial arts for males and females, typing, and speech. Their consensus was that "no courses should be compulsory and a wide variety of electives should be available so a student can take whatever he enjoys and is interested in." They seemed particularly bitter about history, emphasizing that it should be an optional course. "The best education," they concluded, "is got from experiences and not from textbooks."

At the bottom of the student report we tagged on a plaintive plea: "We feel this report should not be taken lightly. We strongly urge that students and teachers of each school enter into meaningful discussion concerning the recommendations contained herein."

"It all seems so futile sometimes," Howard said. The four-man Integrated Studies Committee had retired to a dim corner of the Albatross bar after having worked on the report late into the evening. "You know this report isn't going to do any good. The schools will get the recommendations, ignore them, and grind along as usual."

We sat in glum silence. "Maybe a few kids will see that other people feel the same way they do, that they're not alone," I suggested hopefully.

"The problem is that even in Memorial University they're still training new teachers to perpetuate the old ways," commented Jack Ryan, a recent graduate of Newfoundland's only teacher education institute. "We were lectured and shown that curriculum is something to be followed, not developed or adapted. We were taught how to prepare students for public exams and keep them in line with the threat of grades. Our professors were unapproachable, and education classes were boring and unimaginative. There was little discussion and less room for creativity. How can we expect things to be any different in the schools?"

Ed Randall had been teaching in Newfoundland for eight years, longer than the rest of us combined. "A few years ago I wouldn't have agreed with you," he said, "but over the last couple of years I've seen everything change except the schools. Things are different. We need to develop in kids flexibility and creative problem-solving skills so they can roll with the changes. But the schools are so set, so unyielding. God, we've got a long way to go."

"There's no way we're going to convince all teachers of what we feel," I offered. "Maybe that's not even desirable, I don't know. But more and more kids, parents and teachers are demanding something different from schools now, and the old monopoly system just can't bend enough to meet those divergent demands. They're going to have to open up and provide people with options." I paused and took a drink. "Aren't they?"

194

12

"Two lousy points on a final exam"

While the previous winter had been savage and unpredictable, by March this one just seemed interminable. We had had few of the violent storms that had at least provided some excitement the year before; instead we had been subjected to month after month of unrelieved cold, wind and snow.

The first thaw did not occur until the middle of April. That day I watched the water dripping off the foot-long icicles hanging from our eaves and immediately dashed downstairs to try once more to persuade the water to flow through the plastic pipe that extended through the basement window, looped for twenty feet across the earthen floor and finally coupled with an electric pump.

The water line from our well had not been laid deep enough and as a result had frozen solid in January. Since then, it had continued to defy every attempt at clearing it. In desperation Morgan had hit on the idea of running a second line through the basement window, across the ground and into the well. This had worked great for a few days, but then it too froze. For months we had been forced to haul all our water into the house in buckets.

The first day of the thaw loosened up the above-ground line enough to allow water to be drawn directly from the well for the first time in over three months. Even though it froze again that night, we were elated.

Though winter closed back two days later for an extended engagement, we made sure we kept the water line open, even when it meant leaving every faucet in the house running all night.

While we had been able to use our plumbing only sparingly during the winter, in April the elementary schools became the first buildings in town to be connected to the new community water line. Flush toilets were installed for the first time.

"We got our water today in school," Jan enthused one afternoon. "And we have toilets and even running water in the sinks!"

"Wow," I said, not really able to match her enthusiasm, "that's exciting."

"Well," she retorted, "it is if you've been working with five-year-old kids for nearly two years without water to wash yourself or them. We didn't even have a drinking fountain, you know."

Jan had had to take her students into the bathroom and show them how to use the toilets. "You never think about having to learn something like that," she said, "but most of my kids had never seen a flush toilet before. When I pushed on the handle and the water swirled out, their eyes almost fell out of their heads. All day kids kept disappearing one by one into the bathrooms. I think the toilets were going all day."

A week later she got a new directive. "Since the children have not been using the toilets responsibly," it read, "all teachers are to restrict use. All toilets are to be flushed only by the teachers and only at noon and after school."

"How can I do that?" Jan asked. "Can you imagine what a mess it is after thirty kids have used a toilet for two or three hours?"

In the high school, meanwhile, the situation became somewhat reversed. With the wells being shallow and located in low marshy areas, there was always a potential problem of water contamination. A few years earlier one of the community wells had been condemned when it was discovered that the bacteria count was several times higher than the acceptable limit. Now the same thing occurred in the high school. A health official had visited the school, taken a water sample, and called urgently the next day to order the closing of all water fountains. The water, we were told, was quite literally alive with bacteria of every sort. For the remainder of the year, until the community water line was extended to the high school, we were unable to drink the water and to slake our thirst were totally dependent on the warm pop sold at noon and after school in the canteen.

"Jeez," Kevin complained on hearing the news, "this is as bad as being in Mexico."

Almost since she had left university, Jan had been thinking about returning to finish her teaching degree. As this winter progressed, her plans had become more definite, and shortly after Christmas she had applied for readmittance. After she had been accepted, and knowing how deeply Jan felt about leaving, I reluctantly decided to enter an M.A. program in curriculum at the same faculty. But even though our resignation was a foregone conclusion, the letter was still hard to write. In the end I wrote Russell for both of us.

We thanked the board for having given us the opportunity to teach and learn in Hoberly Cove and for having provided us with its support and ideas. "The kids here are fantastic," I concluded. "Try to give them someone who will 'encourage instead of discourage, interest instead of bore.'"

I drove down to the post office and watched the letter slowly slide down the chute. As it slipped off the end and disappeared I felt hollow and tired, as though I was just completing a marathon race.

The evening after we had sent in our resignation, I found Jan sitting alone on the couch, looking at papers and sniffling. When I asked her what was wrong she handed me a sheaf of handmade cards.

"Why, these are Mother's Day cards. Where did you get them?"

"Oh, some of the kids gave them to me because their families are Jehovah's Witnesses and their mothers wouldn't take them. But others made one for me and one for their mothers."

Whatever misgivings we had about leaving were soon buried under the unrelenting weather. On May 16, we had a snow storm that dumped six inches of snow on the area. Incredulous, I snapped several Polaroid pictures of the SAAB blanketed with snow, and wrote the date on the back.

"I want to make sure to save those," Jan told me, "to show you whenever you talk about coming back."

On May 26 one of the worst blizzards of the winter slammed us, dropping eight inches of snow and closing the schools for the day.

The weather broke on the first of June. We went to sleep in winter and woke up in summer. The leaves, frustrated for months, seemed to explode overnight. The skies cleared, the ice melted.

Like the leaves, the fishermen had been confined by the cold and ice. Now, as the ice cleared, they tried to salvage what they could of the abbreviated lobster season.

The sudden appearance of life and activity in the harbour, and of the area's startling beauty, made our severance from the community even harder. We had become so involved with the town, the school and the kids that it seemed unlikely that we would ever totally separate from it.

Nonetheless, school ground on. Finals became the dominant concern in the high school, especially with the grade elevens, and it seemed ironic that my last interaction with them would be reviewing the writing of a précis. We also spent a period looking at essay titles from past public exams, as one essay question would make up forty per cent of the English language exam. This exam, of course, was totally separate from the three-hour literature exam.

Fortunately, some of the pressure was relieved since we had received final approval for providing half the grade according to class work. "Rank your students," we were instructed via a directive from St. John's, "according to how they compare with the average English student across Newfoundland, not just in your school." I was delighted to be able to provide each student, with one or two exceptions, with at least sixty points towards the combined total of the hundred necessary for a pass. I was afraid that anything more, since the official average mark was a sixty and a fifty per cent failure rate was routine, would jeopardize the formula's use in our school in the future. I just hoped it would be enough.

Jan used the time far more constructively. She had asked for and received a shipment of brightly coloured hula-hoops and, fifteen years after they had swept the rest of North America, they became an instant success in Hoberly Cove. The kids had never heard of hula-hoops, but lost no time in learning how to operate them. Long after school was out for the day I would drive in to pick Jan up and a dozen kids would still be gyrating furiously in the school yard.

Making as much of the warm summer days as possible, she also took her kids on picnics to the point and on hikes along the seacoast.

Though I tried to get my kids out by doing outside writing projects and having them report on various occupations in the community by arranging and recording interviews, some of the excitement was gone. The kids knew we were leaving, and there was a sadness or resignation that seemed to sap our energy.

I dutifully prepared and administered my in-school finals, wished the elevens the best (public exams were not to be held until a week after school had closed), and suddenly it was over. Only the stacks of exams and the charade of grades remained.

On the end of each of my grade nine English exams I had written a final note. "Thank you for a full and wonderful two years. You are fine, capable, sensitive people and, despite my occasional curtness and thoughtlessness, I love you all. Goodbye and good luck to all of you."

Only the replies I got, scribbled after two hours of work on the exam, made the task of marking them bearable. Almost every student had written his own goodbye. One tiny, very shy girl who had never said more than a few words to me in two years wrote nearly half a page. "I enjoyed your teaching us too," she wrote.

"I'm sure we will all miss you—I know I will. I know I'll never pass English, but I'll never forgive you for not giving me a picture of you. I asked for one last year and you said you'd bring one down. Then I asked for one this year. Yesterday, when I didn't get one I could feel a lump in my throat. I would have come up to your house but I had to open up the restaurant after school and worked to 11. But I guess I still love you, and I really enjoyed working with you the last two years."

God, I thought wearily, how fragile. How easy it is to hurt, even for us who are trying not to.

Only the last showdown of the final promotional meeting remained. Again I passed all my students and again I watched helplessly while they were flunked in other classes. But when a girl I had had for two years in English who I thought had become one of the most sensitive writers in the school (the same girl who had written so long ago that the world of school was "rusty and red" during our first trip outside) was flunked for the entire year because she had scored a forty-eight per cent on her math final, I exploded.

This was my last stand and I pulled out the stops.

"You mean to tell me that you're going to deprive this girl of her entire grade nine year because of two lousy points on a final exam?" I yelled.

"It's just a formality," Norman said placatingly. "She'll continue to grade ten; she just won't have her nine certificate."

"A formality? Flunking one of the finest students in the school because she just barely missed passing one exam by two marks is a formality?"

We had clearly reached an impasse. It was obvious that I was not budging and would have to be almost bodily removed before the meeting went on.

Willis, her math teacher, excused himself quietly. A few minutes later he returned: "I went back over Charlene's paper and found two more points. I can pass her now."

Relieved, everyone sat back and rambled on. I watched disconsolately, contributing only now and then. I had won that little skirmish, but so what?

The last week in Hoberly Cove was too hectic to have much impact. Terry Rowe gave us one of his family's trunks, and with the help of the kids we managed to pack all the belongings that we could not coax into the SAAB into three trunks and various boxes we had collected. On the last night, we went to Roger and Judy's house for dinner. They had decided to stay one more year—Roger had found working in special education far more satisfying than his years in the high school. We said goodbye to them and drove back up to the dark house.

As soon as we walked through the door all hell broke loose. Kids sprang from everywhere, screaming "surprise," or just screaming. Our little cassette tape recorder was splitting its speaker, belting out the Rolling Stones at its highest volume, and kids were dancing all over. There must have been sixty students in the house.

Many of them brought small presents (the grade elevens presented me with a framed picture of a Newfoundland dog with their signatures), but all of them had come to let us know we would be missed. The party rollicked along until early morning. The kids we had been closest to said their goodbyes quickly, all our eyes wet, and left quietly, not even yelling a last comment as they walked slowly down the back stairs.

The next morning, the house was as empty and lifeless as we had first found it. Not a single kid was waiting at the door. We had rolled our sleeping bags up and were about to leave when we heard a gentle knock at the door. Morgan, Eileen and their children had come down to see us off. Morgan had on a sweater and an ironed shirt—the first time I had ever seen him dressed up except for Sundays or when he went to a dance. It was a brilliant day with the kind of clear, bright sky that seems almost shocking in Newfoundland. We finished packing, then snapped pictures of each other, and it was time to go.

"We'll take care of shipping your stuff out," Morgan said. "Just let me know where to send it." Then he took my hand and squeezed it softly, "Goodbye, Don, my son."

My throat had swollen shut and I could hardly talk. We climbed into the SAAB and waved at the family standing on our steps.

As we drove for the last time out the little lane that ran by our house to the main road, I thought about Morgan, a man irrevocably a part of, yet also outside of the community he would live in the rest of his life. I thought about the purple school still squatting in the muck, and the town watching itself be transformed. And I thought about the Beothucks.

But most of all I thought about the kids I had taught. What, I wondered, as so many times before, would happen to them?

13

Afterword

During the school year after we left Hoberly Cove, ninety per cent of the students in my former grade nine class either dropped out of school or failed grade ten. Of the thirty grade nines in school at the end of my last year, only three graduated from grade ten. A similarly high dropout failure rate, though not as extreme, occurred in the other grades as well.

Warrick, Kevin and Terry collaborated on a letter to me the fall after we left. "Because of the reputation we've got," they wrote, "Norman has activated the 'War Measures Act.' It gives the new English teacher more power than ever. We didn't do one of her undigestable assignments—we were supposed to pick out something in the sentence, but we didn't know what she was talking about. So Warrick had to see Norman and got a bad report sent home to his parents. Now he's got a bed in the wood house and huddles around a rusty stove. No, boy, that's a fib, but it almost happened. Now by the time you get this letter Lloyd will be expelled because of a showdown with the old battle axe today."

But their problems were not occurring only in English. Warrick sent a history test: "(a) Illustrate and describe the three types of Greek columns. (b) Give as many reasons why the Greeks might have been able to come up with so many beautiful works of art. (c) Discuss the splendid achievements made by Greeks in literature, science, mathematics and art. (d) What are the characteristics of Hellenistic Art?" It was clear that the school was determined to keep teaching the old tired material the old (and ineffectual) way, and any kids who got in the way had to go.

And go they did. By spring nearly half the class was out of school, and Kevin, Lloyd Rowe, Maxwell and Wade Pritchett were in Toronto looking for work. Only Kevin remained in Toronto a year, but as his friends returned to Hoberly and his loneliness increased, he too became disillusioned. His first letters to me from the city were bitter, almost frightened. "I'm an automatic die-cutting machine operator," he wrote. "To put it short I'm a slave on an assembly line where they make bloody old slippers. I'm getting only $2.50 an hour, but I'm going to ask for a raise. I'm also looking for another job because where I'm working they all speak Italian, and you can get in a lot of trouble when you don't know what they're telling you. Today I got into working two hours overtime by just saying 'yes' to something I couldn't understand."

Later he seemed to have adapted somewhat. "I'm over my period of maladjustment. Everything was a burden and I just couldn't cope with the tearing mad rush. But now it's different. All I had to do was make myself at home, get in the same groove and slip along like everyone else." He'd managed to get himself laid off instead of fired (so as to qualify for unemployment insurance benefits sooner), then found a new job where he worked boxing aluminum doors in a plant that was, he said, "forty per cent Newfoundlanders." But a few months later, Kevin too was back in Hoberly Cove.

Nearly all my grade elevens had managed to pass their exams and matriculate. Only one boy failed. But the elevens too found the world a hostile place. Sarah Collins fought her way through two nursing programs, which she found stultifying and unstimulating, before she finally enrolled in an English education program at Memorial. There she gained confidence and began to do extremely well. During this period she wrote me often, describing the situation in Hoberly Cove.

"Most of the class I graduated with are still home doing absolutely nothing," she wrote. "Drugs have hit hard. Not with regard to tragedies, but in the sense that many of the kids depend on it, saying life is so boring for them. A whole lot of the crowd that were in 8th, 9th, and 10th grades when you were here have dropped out of school and they too just laze around. None of them want to stay on in school and I don't blame them. From reports I've been getting on what's going on in there things sure sound pretty dull.

"Anyway, whenever I go home I sure feel sorry for them because they all look so disillusioned with their lives. They actually look blank-eyed and like zombies to me. I feel that they're dissatisfied with their lives and don't know how to go about picking themselves up again. And no wonder, with some of the teachers! They make it appear that life ends at grade 11 when it really only begins."

The next year Kevin went back to school for one more try. While there he led a walkout over the school policy against dances and got interviewed several times by CBC radio in St. John's. And, with Warrick, he started a newspaper. But the pressures against him at school increased and he left school soon after. That year three teachers quit before Christmas. "Rumours have it," one student wrote me, "that the students are the cause, while others say the present teachers crowded out the newcomers. I'm inclined to believe the latter."

205